A Woodland Feast

*Native American Foodways
of the 17th & 18th Centuries*

A Woodland Feast

*Native American Foodways
of the
17th & 18th Centuries*

Carolyn Raine

PENOBSCOT PRESS

All rights reserved
Copyright © 1997 Carolyn Raine
International Standard Book Number 0-89725-309-4
Library of Congress Catalog Card Number 97-67327

No part of this publication may be reproduced, stored in a retrieval system, or transmitted in any form or by any means whatsoever, whether electronic, mechanical, magnetic recording, or photocopying, without the prior written approval of the Copyright holder, excepting brief quotations for inclusion in book reviews.

First Printing June 1997

This book is available from:

Morning Star* Publications
P.O. Box 24414
Huber Heights, Ohio 45424

Cover Illustration: *"Their fitting at meate"*, a Theodor de Bry engraving, c.1590, from an original water-color by John White, painted in 1585, at Roanoke.

Manufactured in the United States of America
Printed on 60# acid-free paper
∞

*This book is dedicated to the loving memory of my Father
Carl L. Beckwith
His faith, love, patience, strength, and courage were always an inspiration. I am thankful to The Creator for our time together.*

TABLE OF CONTENTS

Introduction

Chapter One
    *Meat, Fish & Fowl*_____1
Chapter Two
    *Corn*_____7
Chapter Three
    *Bread*_____11
Chapter Four
    *Beans*_____15
Chapter Five
    *Squash & Pumpkins*_____17
Chapter Six
    *Wild Rice*_____19
Chapter Seven
    *Roots*_____21
Chapter Eight
    *Nuts & Seeds*_____23
Chapter Nine
    *Fruits & Berries*_____25
Chapter Ten
    *Spices & Seasonings*_____27
Chapter Eleven
    *Beverages*_____31
Chapter Twelve
    *European Goods*_____33

Recipes
- *Traditional & Modern* 37
- Helpful Hints 38
- *Meat* 39
- *Jerk* 43
- *Fish* 45
- *Fowl* 47
- *Corn* 48
- *Hominy* 49
- *Parched Corn* 51
- *Popcorn* 52
- *Bread* 53
- *Leaf Bread* 55
- *Beans* 57
- *Squash* 60
- *Pumpkin* 61
- *Wild Rice* 62
- *Roots* 64
- *Nuts* 66
- *Fruits & Berries* 67
- *Spices & Seasonings* 69
- *Beverages* 70

Botanical Names 72
Bibliography 74
Narrative Index 80
Recipe Index 86

SPECIAL THANKS

____To The Creator for blessing us with an abundant harvest.

____To Alan Gutchess, for all his help in putting this book together.

____To Jim O'Neil (and the blizzard of '96), for access to a large amount of research material, and being "snowed in" with it.

____To John Livingston, whose contribution finally brought me into the 20th century.

____To Cleon Grover, for his faith, support and "*corny*" jokes.

____To Family and Friends, for all their encouragement.

____To all those who have been my willing (*or not*) "guinea pigs" at trying some new, "old" food things.

INTRODUCTION

This book is based on primary source documentation, from over one hundred original 17th and 18th century journals, captivity narratives, and ethnobotanical research. With "field tested" recipes it is, basically, a historical cookbook.

Since most Native traditions were oral, we must be grateful to those early writers who thought it important enough to give us the details of their experiences and observations. In one way we are given a look into the lives and customs of ordinary people who took the gifts that the Creator provided and made them into useful, as well as, beautiful things.

I have been a reenactor for the last fifteen years and a historian all my life. I am constantly trying to find new insight into how my ancestors lived, before the coming of the Europeans; and what changes were made by the introduction of foreign products.

Most of the food items are indigenous to Eastern North America, although one must realize that some common plants, in fact, originated in South America. These were brought north in prehistoric times. By the 15th century many plants were already growing wild, as well as, being cultivated.

I have also included a chapter on European introduced goods that were readily adapted by the Native people.

For those of you who do "living history" imagine this: You have spent years and a great deal of money, researching your persona. You've poured over countless books and old paintings to come up with the correct clothes and accouterments. You have a camp to be proud of at any historical event. You look down into your beautiful, handcarved, wooden bowl, and come face to face with "beans & wieners"!! What is wrong with this picture?

For years it seems that historically accurate foods are the last thing that people consider as a part of reenacting. I am sure most have avoided this because they have no idea what to cook; they think it may be too difficult; or bland tasting. Well...some of that is true, but much depends upon your taste, and what you are willing to do to be authentic. However, take heart, I have found many foods that are easy to prepare, and they taste good.

The incredible variety of plants and animals that were available, and the combinations that our Grandmothers came up with, were quite ingenious. Many foods that we consider "gourmet" today, were, at that time, the staples of almost every Native diet.

Mary Rowlandson 1676...they would eat, all sorts of wild birds which they could catch; also bear, venison, beavers, tortoise, frogs, squirrels, dogs, skunks, rattlesnakes, yea the very bark of trees...*pg.54*

James Adair 1747...they kill wild game, fish, fresh water tortoises, gather a plentiful variety of vegetables, and live in affluence...*pg.322*

Peter Kalm 1749...beavers, bears, reindeer, elks, hares, and several kinds of birds. Those Indians who live far southward, eat the following things. Of vegetables they plant corn, wild kidney beans of several kinds, pumpkin of different sorts, squashes, a kind of gourd...and melons. All these plants have been cultivated by the Indians long before the arrival of the Europeans. They likewise eat various fruits which grow in their woods. Fish and meat constitute a very large part of their food. And they like chiefly the flesh of wild cattle [*buffalo*], roe-bucks, stags, bears, beavers and some other quadrupeds. Among their dainty dishes they reckon the water taregrass [*wild rice*]...*pg.533*

J. Heckewelder 1770...the principal food of the Indians consists of the game which they take or kill in the woods, the fish out of the waters, and the maize, potatoes, beans, pumpkins, squashes, cucumbers, melons...they make use also of various roots of plants, fruits, nuts, and berries out of the woods, by way of relish or as a seasoning to their victuals, sometimes also from necessity...*pg.193*

The general "rule of thumb" for any meal was, whatever game could be had, whatever vegetables, roots, nuts, or berries were in season, all went into the pot !

The question of food "taboos" does arise periodically. I have found that, historically, on many occasions, what one tribe refuses to eat, another will, and even within a particular tribe, it becomes personal preference (i.e.: one would not eat one's own totem or clan symbol). There was no absolute right or wrong.

Many people are curious about regular meal times and winter food preservation.

There were no set times for specific meals. There would always be food available, day or night, for whoever was hungry.

Col. James Smith 1755...they have no such thing as regular meals, breakfast, dinner, or supper; but if any one, even the town [*village*] folks, would go to the same house several times in one day, he would be invited to eat of the best--and with them it is bad manners to refuse to eat when it is offered. If they will not eat, it is interpreted as a symptom of displeasure, or that the persons refusing to eat, were angry with those who invited them...*pg154*.

On preserving food for the winter: It was not done on a scale as we would expect. They did dry and store a few things, but for the most part, they relied on their faith in the Creator to provide for them as they needed.

J. Heckewelder 1770...the woods and waters, at certain times and seasons, furnish to the Indians an abundant supply of wholesome nourishing food, which, if carefully gathered, cured and stored up, would serve them for the whole year, so that none need perish or even suffer from hunger; but they are not accustomed to laying in stores of provisions, except some Indian corn, dry beans and a few other articles. Hence they are sometimes reduced to great straits, and not seldom in absolute want of necessaries of life, especially in the time of war. Yet, notwithstanding the numerous famines they have been visited with,...the Indians will support themselves in the midst of the greatest difficulties, never despairing of their fate, but trusting to their exertions, and to the protection of the Almighty Being who created them...*pg.198*

This is, by no means, a *complete* list of traditional foods and recipes. There were many options depending on what part of the country you lived in, and what meat, vegetables, etc. were in season. This is only a broad look at the most basic foods that were common in the 17th and 18th centuries.

I hope that this book will encourage those cooks who would like to try traditional Native American foods; and if cooking is not your forte, you will find the historical information interesting.

CHAPTER ONE

MEAT, FISH & FOWL

The most important food source was the wild game that abounded in the forests, the rivers and the skies: Buffalo, bear, deer, elk, moose, beaver, raccoon, rabbit, and squirrel; fish, turtle, crawfish, mussels, and clams; turkey, pheasant, duck, goose, pigeon, and their eggs. These were the most common, but many other animals, birds, and reptiles were also eaten.

The methods of food preparation were roasting or broiling over an open fire; boiling, often making a soup or stew; and drying, also known as "jerk", which was important for preserving food for use on the trail and through the winter.

Col. James Smith 1755...this with us was called good living, though not equal to our fat, roasted, and boiled venison, when we went to the woods in the fall; or bears meat and beaver in the winter; or sugar, bears oil, and dry venison in the spring...*pg.159*
...had plenty of fat venison, bears meat and raccoons...*pg.142*
...one of the bears was very large and remarkably fat. The hunters carried in meat sufficient to give us all a hearty supper and breakfast...*pg.143*
...they gave me plenty of fat beaver meat...*pg.171*
Alexander Henry 1760...the principal animals which the country afforded were the stag or red deer, the common American deer, the bear, raccoon, beaver and marten, all of which we hunted through the months of cold and snow...*pg.89*
...*[after killing a bear]* the skin being taken off, we found the fat in several places six inches deep, this loaded two persons, and the flesh parts were as much as four persons could carry...*pg.94*

Dr. Knight 1782...having gone about three miles found a deer which had been recently killed. The meat was sliced from the bones and bundled up in the skin...*pg.6*

John Tanner 1789...we found beavers, also some otters and muskrats. We had brought with us some corn and grease so that, with the fish we caught, and the game we killed, we lived comfortably...*pg.22*

...I had now become aquainted with the method of taking rabbits in snares...*pg.48*

Quintin Stockwell 1677...they lit of a moose and killed it, and staid there till they had eaten it all up...*pg.64*

Elizabeth Hanson 1724...catch a squirrel or beaver, and at other times we met with nuts, berries, and roots which they digged out of the ground...*pg.117*

O.M. Spencer 1792...partake of the plentiful feast...consisting of boiled jerk and fish, stewed squirrels and venison, and green corn boiled, some in the ear, and some cut from the cob and mixed with beans, besides squashes and roasted pumpkins...*pg.99*

Benjamin Gilbert 1780...towards evening the parties again met and encamped, having killed a deer, they kindled a fire, each one roasting pieces of the flesh upon sharpened switches...*pg.74*

J. Heckewelder 1770...their meat they either boil, roast, or broil. Their roasting is done by running a wooden spit through the meat, sharpened at each end, which they place near the fire, and occasionally turn. They broil on clean coals, drawn off from the fire for that purpose...*pg.196*

Col. James Smith 1755...we remained at this camp about eight or ten days, and killed a number of deer. Though we had neither bread nor salt at this time, yet we had both roast and boiled meat in great plenty...*pg.134*

...a young Ground Hog, about as large as a Rabbit, roasted..*pg.122*

James Adair 1747...all his war store of provisions consisted in three stands of barbicued venison...*pg.316*

Col. James Smith 1755...I immediately hung on the kettle with some water, and cut the beef [*buffalo*] in thin slices, and put them in...when it had boiled awhile...*pg.195*

Benjamin Gilbert 1780...one of the Indians...returned with a large piece of meat, ordering the captives to boil it...*pg.83*

Quintin Stockwell 1677...they had killed an otter, and gave me some of the broth made of it, and a bit of the flesh...*pg.65*

Col. James Smith 1755...I went along...and killed a buffaloe. When this was done, we jirked the lean, and fryed the tallow out of the fat meat, which we kept to stew with our jirk as we needed it...*pg.214*

Peter Henry 1780...the Indians killed a bear and two does that day...they brought the meat of all to the camp that evening, and some of them was busily engaged in cutting the meat off the bones and drying it on a little rod or stick over the fire to make what the Indians call Jerk--dried meat to carry with them...*pg.36*

...one of the Indians...attended...continually throughout the night to drying their meat, making Jerk of it so as to carry it with them...*pg.38*

John Tanner 1789...the women, finding that the elk was large and fat, determined on remaining to dry the meat before they carried it home...*pg.41*

Alexander Henry 1760...we remained two days, drying the meat. The method was to cut it into slices of the thickness of a steak and then hang it over the fire, in the smoke...*pg.90*

...we were soon in possession of four thousand pounds of dried venison...*pg.95*

Capt. Spencer Records 1784...we skinned the bull [*buffalo*], and cut off all the meat in broad thin pieces, which we laid on the hide, and sprinkled salt thereon, letting it lay till we made a long [*burning*] fire. We then put a row of forks on each side of the fire, and placed poles on the forks. Small sticks were then laid on them, and the meat laid on the sticks over the fire, where it remained until half cooked; it was then turned over and left to lay till morning, for by this time it was in the night...In the morning we put the meat in bags and carried it home...*pg.64*

Benjamin Gilbert 1780...amused himself with catching fish in the lake, and furnished the family with frequent messes of various kinds, which they eat without bread or salt...*pg.118*

...they caught some fish and made soup of them...*pg.125*

...a fish called "*Ozoondah*", resembling a shad in shape, but rather thicker and less bony, with which lake Erie abounded, were often dressed for their table, and were of an agreeable taste, weighing from three to four pounds...*pg.126*

John Gyles 1689...an Indian feast--the ingredients are fish, flesh or Indian corn, and beans boiled together...*pg.98*

Col. James Smith 1755...here we diverted ourselves several days, by catching rock-fish [*large mouth bass*] in a small creek...*pg.200*

...the rock-fish here, when they begin first to run up the creek to spawn, are exceedingly fat, and sufficient to fry themselves.*pg.201*

...he sat with his net, and when he felt the fish touch the net he drew it up, and frequently would haul out two or three rock-fish that would weigh about five or six pounds each...*pg.201*

H.M. van den Bogaert 1634...three women came here from the *Sinnekens* [*Senecas*] with some dried and fresh salmon...*pg.6*

...in this river, there are six or seven or even 800 salmon caught in one day. I saw houses with 60, 70 and more dried salmon...*pg.13*

...I bought four dried salmon and two pieces of bear's meat that was nine inches thick; there was some here even thicker...*pg.18*

...we still had five pieces of salmon and two pieces of bear's meat to eat on the way, and we were given here some bread and meal to take along...*pg.19*

John Tanner 1789...we had brought with us one of the nets used about Mackinac, and setting this, the first night, caught about eighty trout and white fish...*pg.22*

...we found more gull's eggs than we were able to take away. We also took, with spears, two or three sturgeons...*pg.25*

John Slover 1782...I got two small crawfish to eat...*pg.32*

Major Moses Van Campen 1778...where a great number of Indian families had come to catch young pigeons...*pg.116*

Elizabeth Hanson 1724...having shot some wild ducks...*pg.120*

Col. James Smith 1755...the hunters came in, who had killed only two small turkeys...*pg.143*

...in this manner we lived, until October; then the geese, swans, ducks, cranes, etc. came from the north, and alighted on this little Lake, innumerable...*pg.159*

...they gave us plenty of homony, and wild fowl, boiled and roasted. As the geese, ducks, swans, etc. here are well grain-fed, they were remarkably fat...*pg.161*

Thomas Brown 1757...finally I was allowed a gun to kill pigeons, which were very plentiful here. I shot a number, split and dried them...*pg.71*

Benjamin Gilbert 1780...an Indian came with an account that an astonishing number of young pigeons might be procured at a certain place by falling trees that were filled with nests of young...which they dried in the sun and with smoke, and filled several bags...*pg.130*

John Tanner 1789...the [*turkey*] nest contained a number of eggs...they [*Indians*] immediately took the eggs from me, and kindling a fire, put them in a small kettle to boil...*pg.6*

I have included here, a few of the more "unusual" meals. I hope you find them as amusing as I did.

John Tanner 1789...we could eat only the tongue [*of the buffalo*]...*pg.49*

Hugh Gibson 1756...sometimes they catch a number of frogs, and hang them up to dry, when a deer is killed they will split up the guts and give them a plunge or two in the water, and then dry them, and when they run out of provisions, they will take some of the dryed frogs, and some of the deers guts and boil them, till the flesh of the frogs is dissolved, they then sup the broth...*pg.183* [*frog sausage!*]

Col. James Smith 1755...being very hungry we kindled a fire, opened the bear, took out the liver, and wrapped some of the caul fat round, and put it on a wooden spit, which we stuck in the ground by the fire to roast; we then skinned the bear, got on our kettle, and had both roast and boiled, and also sauce to our meat, which appeared to me to be delicate fare...*pg.145*

Charles Johnston 1790...we regaled ourselves upon the flesh of the [*bear*] cubs. To me it was excellent eating, although the manner of dressing would hardly suit a delicate taste. The entrails were taken out and, after the hair was thoroughly singed from the carcasses, they were roasted whole...*pg.195*

O.M. Spencer 1792...a large hawk...was brought down with the rifle, and being dressed by plucking out the larger, and singeing off the smaller feathers, and then boiled in our brass kettle with a quantity of milkweed, in about half an hour [??] furnished us a dinner of flesh, soup, and greens...*pg.69*

Robert Eastburn 1756...our kettle was put over the fire with some pounded Indian corn, and after it had boiled about two hours, my oldest Indian brother, returned with a she beaver, big with young, which he soon cut to pieces, and threw it into the kettle, together with the guts, and took the four young beavers, whole as they came out of the dam and put them likewise into the kettle and when all was well boiled, gave each one of us a large dishful of the broth, of which we eat freely, and then part of the old beaver, the tail of which was divided equally among us; the four young beavers were cut in the middle, and each of us got half of a beaver...*pg.29*

...the other Indians catched young muskrats, run a stick through their bodies, and roasted, without being skinned or gutted, and so eat them...*pg.29*

Susanna Johnson 1754...the evening was employed in drying and smoking what remained [*of the horse meat*] for future use...*pg.61*

...our supper consisted of gruel and the broth of a hawk they had killed the preceding day...*pg.60*

Mary Rowlandson 1676...in the morning they took the blood of the deer, and put it into the paunch, and so boiled it...*pg.43* [*blood pudding!*]

CHAPTER TWO

CORN

The most common vegetable crops were corn, beans, and squash. Referred to by some as "the Three Sisters", these were the basis of almost every meal.
Corn, or maize, came in many varieties: soft, also known as bread corn, 8 rowed flint, dent, and even popcorn. These also came in many colors: white, yellow, red, black, purple or blue, and calico or multi-colored. Green corn, refers to fresh corn in the milk stage, not the color.
When it comes to ingenuity, this is where the Grandmothers could have written their own book, "Corn: 1001 ways!". They boiled it, roasted it, dried it, parched it, pounded it into meal, and boiled it with wood ashes to make hominy.

Peter Williamson 1754...they would sometimes give me a little meat, but my chief food was Indian corn...*pg.83*
John M'Cullough 1756...the most of the Indians of the town [*village*] were either at their corn-fields or out a fishing...*pg.261*
Benjamin Gilbert 1780...this family raised this summer about one hundred skipple of Indian corn (a skipple is about three pecks) equal to seventy-five bushels...*pg.125*
Thomas Hariot 1586...[*on corn varieties*] some white, some red, some yellow and some blew...
O.M. Spencer 1792...feast them principally on green corn, variously cooked...*pg.95*
...about the middle of August, when the ears of corn, grown to full size, were yet in that soft milky state in which they are used for roasting...*pg.94*

Col. James Smith 1755...they gave me also a bowl and wooden spoon, which I carried with me to the place, where there was a number of large brass kettles full of boiled venison and green corn...*pg131*

John M'Cullough 1756...when their corn is in the roasting-ear...they boil the whole in their kettles, and take as much of the green corn as they judge to be sufficient for their purpose, scraping it off the cob, and thickening the broth with it...*pg.288*

J. Heckewelder 1770...the Indians have a number of manners of preparing their corn. They make an excellent pottage of it, by boiling it with fresh or dried meat (the latter pounded), dried pumpkins, dry beans, and chestnuts. They sometimes sweeten it with sugar or molasses from the sugar-maple tree. Another very good dish is prepared by boiling with their corn or maize, the washed kernels of the shell-bark or hickory nut...*pg.194*

...his wife has pounded her corn, now boiling on the fire, and baked her bread, which gives them a good breakfast...*pg.194*

Alexander Henry 1760...he asked everyone, by turn, for his dish and put into each two boiled ears of maize...*pg.90*

Col. James Smith 1755...we had with us green corn, which we roasted and ate that night...*pg.133*

...about the time that these warriors came in, the green corn was beginning to be of use, so that we had either green corn or venison, and sometimes both--which was, comparatively, high living. When we could have plenty of green corn, or roasting ears [*corn on the cob*]...*pg.158*

James Adair 1747...we alighted at a cool stream of water, to smoke and drink corn-flour and water, according to our usual custom in the woods...*pg.331*

Mary Rowlandson 1676...I carried, two quarts of parched meal ...*pg.30*

Col. James Smith 1755...all that we had then to live on was corn pounded into coarse meal or small homony--this they boiled in water, which appeared like well thickened soup...*pg.157*

Mary Jemison 1755...our cooking consisted in pounding our corn into samp or hominy, boiling the hominy, making now and then a cake and baking it in the ashes, and in boiling or roasting our venison...*pg.72*

J. Heckewelder 1770...their *Psindamo'can* or *Tassmana'ne*, as they call it, is the most nourishing and durable food made out of the Indian corn. The blue sweetish kind is the grain which they prefer for that purpose. They parch it in clean hot ashes, until it bursts, it is then sifted and cleaned, and pounded in a mortar into a kind of flour, and when they wish to make it very good, they mix some sugar with it. When wanted for use, they take about a table spoonful of this flour in their mouths, then stopping to the river or brook, drink water to it. If, however, they have a cup or other small vessel at hand, they put the flour in it and mix it with water, in proportion of one table spoonful to a pint. At their camps they will put a small quantity in a kettle with water and let it boil down, and they will have a thick pottage. With this food, the traveller and warrior will set out on long journeys and expeditions, and as a little of it will serve them for a day, they have not a heavy load of provisions to carry. Persons who are unacquainted with this diet ought to be careful not to take too much at a time, and not to suffer themselves to be tempted too far by its flavour; more than one or two spoonfuls at most at any one time or at one meal is dangerous; for it is apt to swell in the stomach or bowels, as when heated over a fire...*pg.195*

Benjamin Gilbert 1780...pounding hommony was this days' employment...they boiled and pounded it for supper...*pg.84*

...the kettle was again set on the fire, for hommony, this being their only food...*pg.85*

O.M. Spencer 1792...gave us first some boiled hommony, and then a little corn cake and boiled venison...*pg.71*

I have included this next story for three reasons: It gives a good description of how hominy was made, it shows how cleanliness was important (even in a rustic environment), and it conjures up quite a funny image. DO NOT TRY THIS AT HOME!!

O.M. Spencer 1792...[*the old woman*] was remarkably nice in her cookery; requiring her kettles to be scoured often, and her bowls and spoons to be washed daily, and nothing offended her quicker than the appearance of sluttishness; and although I stood pretty high in her favour, I sometimes incurred her displeasure by my neglect, particularly by my want of cleanliness, as she thought, in performing some of my household duties. On a very cold morning, about the middle of January, she had risen before day, and intending to make some hommony, had boiled the corn for some time with the ashes to remove its hulls. It was my duty to cleanse it from the ashes, and as it had been long enough in them, I was ordered to get up and perform that duty. The old woman's temper was very quick, and when roused, she was like a fury; and by no means particular in selecting an instrument of punishment, when her poker was not at hand, seized a knife, axe billet of wood, anything within her reach, hurling it at the unfortunate subject of her wrath. Not rising immediately, she uttered her customary *Oogh!* followed by a stroke of her poker, and not giving me time to put on my moccasons, hurried me off with the kettle of boiling corn and a large coarse sieve to the river. The Maumee had for some time been frozen over, and through the ice, about six inches thick, we had cut and kept open a hole for the convenience of getting water. Placing the large sieve by the side of the opening, and emptying the corn in it, I proceeded to dig up water, pouring it on the hommony, which I rubbed well to take off the hulls. I had not finished my work when my bare feet, all this time standing on the ice, were so pained with the cold that I could endure it no longer, and stepping into the hommony, was enjoying the luxury of its warmth when the old woman espied me.---Calling me loudly by my Indian name, *Mechee-way*, and uttering several *ooghs*, she ran down furious with rage to the river, and hurling her poker, inflicted a severe blow on my back, felling me to the ice. Immediately, however, springing up, I ran off, leaving her to finish the hommony, and did not return to the cabin until her anger had subsided...*pg.113*

CHAPTER THREE

BREAD

The basic Native bread was corn, or hominy, fresh or dried, pounded into a meal and mixed with water. This was made into small cakes that were either baked in hot ashes (ash cakes) or dropped into boiling water, soup, or stew, to make boiled corn bread, or dumplings. The cornmeal was also wrapped in corn husks and boiled, similar to Mexican tamales.

<u>George Percy 1607</u>...I saw Bread made by their women, which doe all their drugerie...The manner of baking bread is thus. After they pound their wheate [*maize*] into flour, with hote water they make it into paste, and worke it into round balls and Cakes; then they put it into a pot of seething water; when it is sod thoroughly, they lay it on a smooth stone, there they harden it as well as in an oven...*pg.69*

...the meanest sort brought us such dainties as they had, and of their bread which they make of their Maiz or Gennea wheat. They would not suffer us to eat unless we sate down, which we did on a mat right against them...*pg.63*

<u>Col. James Smith 1755</u>...we had now plenty of homony and the best of fowls; and sometimes we had a little bread made of Indian corn meal, pounded in a homony-block, mixed with boiled beans, and baked in cakes under the ashes...*pg.159*

<u>H.M. van den Bogaert 1634</u>...a small loaf of bread baked with beans...*pg.3*

<u>John M'Cullough 1756</u>...pounds a mortar full of corn, bakes it into cakes...*pg.295*

John M'Cullough 1756...they generally select their seed corn, when they are pulling it. After they plant, they take part of what is left, and sometimes the whole, and pounds it into meal, then kneads it into a large cake, and bakes it under the ashes...*pg.159*
Benjamin Gilbert 1780...had brought with them cakes of hommony and Indian corn; of this they made a good meal...*pg.84*
Susanna Johnson 1754...for supper they made more porridge and some johnny cakes. My portion was brought me in a little bark...*pg.59*
Benjamin Gilbert 1780...had brought with them cakes of hommony and Indian corn; of this they made a good meal...*pg.84*
John M'Cullough 1756...homony, or dumplings, made of coarse Indian meal boiled in water...*pg.261*
Peter Kalm 1749...sometimes the pulp [*of pumpkins*] is kneaded into a dough with maize; of this they make pancakes...*pg.517*

Here is another funny story.
(Native people have always had a great sense of humor).

Peter Henry 1780...one of them was very expert in cooking and turning pancakes. He had a long-handled pan that they took from my father's and he had the batter mixed up and would pour it into the pan, which was swimming in gravy and grease, as they had plenty of bear meat and fat. That night this Indian would swing round the cake in the pan---then he would throw it up and turn the cake out of the pan, and would catch the cake again in the pan and when it would fall back into the pan again, it would make the grease and fat fly all around, which afforded during the cooking operation a great deal of laughing and sport, as the mode of turning the cakes and making the grease fly round was likely new to them. One or two of them [*who*] was sitting mending their moccasins near the fire, and the cook, suffered the most in the scalding scattered grease from the cook's exploits in turning the pancakes...*pg.37*

James Adair 1747...they have another sort of boiled bread which is mixed with beans or potatoes; they put on the soft corn till it begins to boil and pound it sufficiently fine;--their invention does not reach the use of any kind of milk. When the flour is stirred, and dried by the heat of the sun or fire, they sift it with sieves of different sizes...the thin cakes mixt with bear's oil, were formerly baked on thin broad stones placed over a fire, or on broad earthen bottoms fit for such a use, but now they use kettles. When they intend to bake great loaves, they make a strong blazing fire... when it is burnt down to coals they carefully rake them off to each side, and sweep away the remaining ashes; then they put their well kneaded bread loaf, first steeped in hot water, over the hearth, and an earthen basin above it, with the embers of coals atop...when they take it off they wash the loaf with warm water, and it soon becomes firm and very white...*pg.407*

O.M. Spencer 1792...for bread, beside that prepared in the ordinary way from corn meal, we had some made of the green corn, cut from the cob and pounded in a mortar until it was brought to the consistency of thick cream, then being salted and poured into a sort of mold of an oblong form, more than half the length and twice the thickness of a man's hand, made of corn leaves, and baked in the ashes, was very palatable...*pg.99*

J. Heckewelder 1770...their bread is of two kinds; one made up of green corn while in the milk, and another of the same grain when fully ripe and quite dry. The last is pounded as fine as possible, then sifted and kneaded into dough, and afterwards made up into cakes of six inches in diameter and about an inch thickness, rounded off on the edge. In baking these cakes, they are extremely particular; the ashes must be clean and hot, and if possible come out of good dry oak barks, which they say gives a brisk and durable heat. In the dough of this kind of bread, they frequently mix boiled pumpkins, green [*fresh*] or dried, dry beans, or well pared chestnuts, boiled in the same manner, dried venison well pounded, whortleberies [*blueberries*], green [*fresh*] or dry, but not boiled, sugar and other palatable ingredients. For the other kind of bread, the green corn is either pounded or mashed, is put in broad green corn blades, generally filled in with a ladle well wrapped up, and baked in the ashes, like the other. They consider this as a very delicate morsel, but to me it is too sweet...*pg.195*

CHAPTER FOUR

BEANS

Beans were available in both shelled and edible pod varieties: Cranberry, navy, marrow, several types of kidney beans, also known as haricot beans, and green "snap" or "string" beans. These were boiled with meat, or vegetables. They were also mixed into cornmeal to make cakes and dumplings. Beans were very often dried and preserved for winter use.

Father Lafitau 1724...besides maize, they sow horse beans or little lima [*navy?*] beans, pumpkins of a species different from those of France, watermelons, and great sunflowers. They sow the lima [*navy?*] beans next to the grains of their Indian corn, the cane or stalk of which serves them as support as the elm does to the vine...*pg.55*
Jno. Josselyn 1663...[*beans which were*] white, black, red, yellow, blue, spotted...and the kidney bean...
Robert Eastburn 1756...gave us boiled corn and beans to eat...*pg.27*
H.M. van den Bogaert 1634...today we feasted on two bears, and we recieved today one half skipple of beans...*pg.10*
...today we ate beans cooked with bear's meat...*pg.18*
Mary Jemison 1755...the whole company partake of a dinner in common, consisting of meat, corn and beans, boiled together in large kettles, and stirred till the whole is completely mixed and soft...*pg.228*
Col. James Smith 1755...they also gave us what they call "*Caneheanta*", which is a kind of homony, made of green corn, dried, and beans mixed together...*pg.138*

Capt. Gabriel Archer 1607...this night we went some--mile, and ankored at a place I called "Kynd womans care" which is--mile from "Mulbery shade". Here we came within night, yet was there ready for us of bread new made, sodden wheate [*maize*] and beans, mullberyes, and some fishe undressed more than we could eate...*pg.49*

Mary Rowlandson 1676...they were boiling corn and beans...*pg.45*

O.M. Spencer 1792...set before us some refreshment, consisting of dried green corn boiled with beans and dried pumpkins, and making, as I thought, a very excellent dish...*pg.86*

Zadock Steele 1780...we found a few beans...we took and parched them, as we would corn, by the fire...*pg.136*

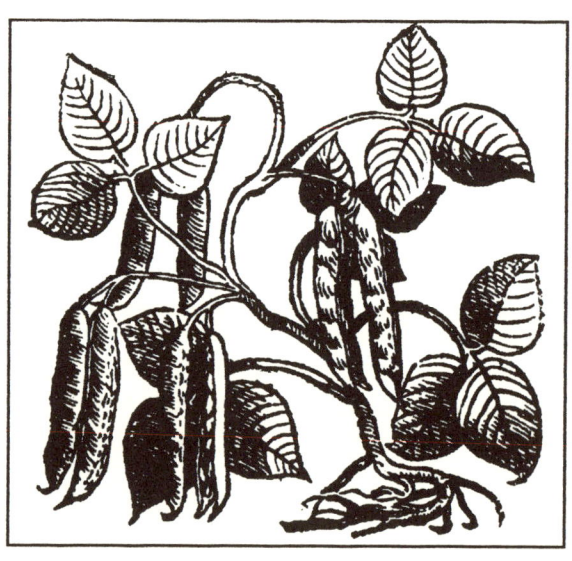

CHAPTER FIVE

SQUASH & PUMPKINS

The last part of "the Three Sisters" is squash: Scalloped, yellow straightneck, yellow crookneck, and green (zucchini) were the summer varieties. The fall offered acorn squash and pumpkins. These were boiled, baked or roasted near the fire, or sliced and dried.

Benjamin Gilbert 1780...they therefore undertook to clear a piece of land, in which they put corn, pumpkins and squashes...*pg.118*
...this being the time for feasting on their new crops of corn, and they having plenty of pumpkins and squashes...*pg.145*
John M'Cullough 1756...we got some squashes to eat...*pg.257*
H.M. van den Bogaert 1634...ate large quantities of pumpkin, beans, and venison...*pg.4*
...we ate here many baked and boiled pumpkins...*pg.4*
J. Heckewelder 1770...they also prepare a variety of dishes from the pumpkin, the squash, and the green French or kidney beans; they are very particular in their choice of pumpkins and squashes, and in their manner of cooking them. The women say that the less water is put to them, the better dish they make, and that it would be still better if they were stewed without any water, merely in the steam of the sap which they contain. They cover up the pots in which they cook them with large leaves of the pumpkin vine...*pg.194*
Peter Kalm 1749...the squashes are commonly boiled, then crushed (as we are used to do with turnips when we make a porridge of them) and seasoned with some pepper or other spice, whereupon the dish is ready...*pg.74*

Peter Kalm 1749...pumpkins are prepared for eating in various ways. The Indians boil them whole, or roast them in ashes and eat them...they have, indeed, a very fine flavor when roasted...*pg.517*

...slice them and put the slices before the fire to roast; when they are done they generally put sugar on the pulp...*pg.517*

...they [*squash*] are eaten boiled, either with meat or by themselves...*pg.183*

...[*pumpkin or squash*] are cut in slices, drawn upon a thread, and dried. They keep all year long, and are then boiled or stewed. All sorts of pumpkins are prepared for eating in different manners...*pg.183*

...the Indians, in order to preserve the pumpkins for a very long time, cut them in long slices which they fasten or twist together and dry either in the sun or by the fire in a room. When they are thus dried, they will keep for years, and when boiled they taste very well. The Indians prepare them thus at home and on their journeys...sometimes they do not take the time to boil the pumpkin, but eat it dry with dried beef or other meat; and I own they are eatable in that state, and very welcome to a hungry stomach...*pg.517*

Besides eating, some found other uses for pumpkins!

Col. James Smith 1755...as he passed me, I hit him with a piece of a pumpkin----which pleased the Indians much, but hurt my feelings...*pg.158* [*FOOD FIGHT!*]

CHAPTER SIX

WILD RICE

Along with corn, beans and squash; wild rice was a staple of the Northern and Great Lakes Native people. Used in much the same way; it was boiled with meat, vegetables, nuts or berries. Often used as trail rations, it was dried and parched.

Wild rice was such an important commodity, that large quantities were packaged in basket-like containers and traded amongst different tribes on a regular basis.

Louis Hennepin 1680...the Indians gave us some wild Oats [*wild rice*] to eat...in great Dishes made of Birch-trees; and the Savage Women season'd them with Bluez [*blueberries*]. This is a sort of Black Grain, which they dry in the Sun in the Summer, and are as good as Corrans [*currants*]...

Peter Kalm 1749...the water taregrass (Zizania Aquatica L.) grows plentifully in their lakes, in stagnant waters, and sometimes in rivers which flow slowly. They gather the seeds in October, and prepare them in different ways, and chiefly as groats, which taste almost as good as rice...*pg.533*

Pierre Radisson 1661...for each man a handful of that [*wild rice*] they putt in the pott, that swells so much that it can suffice a man...

Col. James Smith 1755...the wild fowl here feed upon a kind of wild rice that grows spontaneously in the shallow water...*pg.161*

CHAPTER SEVEN

ROOTS

Root type foods also played an important role in the Native diet. These included wild onions, ground nuts, arrowhead or "swamp potato", wild leeks, cattails, and Jerusalem artichokes (the roots of a type of sunflower). The methods of preparation were boiling or roasting. Certain roots, like groundnuts, arrowhead, and Jerusalem artichokes, were also dried and pounded into a type of flour.

Col. James Smith 1755...they gave us a kind of rough, brown potatoes, which grew spontaneously and were called by the *Caughnewagas "ohnenata"*. These potatoes peeled and dipped in racoon's fat, taste nearly like our sweet potatoes...*pg.138*
John M'Cullough 1756...we have subsisted the greater part of our time on a certain kind of root that has something of the resemblance of a potatoe...*pg.283*
Benjamin Gilbert 1780...to dig up a root, something resembling potatoes, which the Indians call *"whappanies"*...*pg.82*
...they fixed their station near the Genesee banks, and procured more of the wild potatoe roots before mentioned, for their supper...*pg.83*
...when they arrived at their settlement, it was the time of gathering their crop of corn, potatoes, and pumpkins...*pg.128*
Mary Rowlandson 1676...their chief and commonest food was ground-nuts, they eat also nuts and acorns, artichokes, lilly roots, ground beans, and several other weeds and roots...*pg.54*
...some found ears of Indian corn, some found groundnuts...*pg.32*
...a mess of venison and ground-nuts...*pg.42*

Jackson Johonnet 1791...I had not tasted anything except wild berries and ground nuts for above a week...*pg.96*

T. Jefferson 1780...long potatoes, pumpkins of various kinds, and squashes, were also found in use among them...*pg.223*

Peter Kalm 1749...*Hopniss* [*groundnuts*] was the Indian name of a wild plant, which they ate at that time...the roots resemble potatoes, and are boiled by the Indians, who eat them instead of bread...the Indians not only eat these roots, which have as good taste as potatoes, but likewise take the peas which lie in the pods of this plant, and prepare them like common peas...*Katniss* [*arrowhead*] is another Indian name of a plant, the root of which they were also accustomed to eat...the Indians either boiled this root or roasted it in hot ashes...*pg.259*

...they planted but little corn, for they lived chiefly by hunting, and throughout the greatest part of the summer *Hopniss* [*groundnuts*], *Katniss* [*arrowhead*]...and whortleberries [*blueberries*] were their chief food...*pg.269*

James Adair 1747...they are acquainted with a great many herbs and roots...*pg.322*

Benjamin Gilbert 1780...and made a soup of wild onions and turnip tops...*pg.83*

Susanna Johnson 1754...at dusk they made some porridge, and brought a cup to steep some roots in...*pg.59*

Mary Rowlandson 1676...a kettle of ground-nuts boiling...I asked her to let me boil my piece of bear in the kettle, which she did, and gave me some ground-nuts to eat with it; and I cannot but think how pleasant it was to me...*pg.36*

...she gave me a mess of broth which was thickened with meal made of the bark of a tree, and to make it better she had put into it about a handful of peas, and a few roasted ground-nuts...*pg.37*

Zadock Steele 1780...we dug roots of various kinds and ate them, which we roasted by the fire...*pg.137*

Mary Rowlandson 1676...she gave me a mess of beans and meat, and a little ground-nut cake...*pg.46*

CHAPTER EIGHT

NUTS & SEEDS

Many kinds of nuts and seeds were gathered from the forests and fields: Black walnuts, hazelnuts, chestnuts, hickory nuts, beechnuts, and acorns were a few; along with sunflower, squash, and pumpkin seeds. These were eaten raw or roasted, or added to cooked foods. They were also pounded into a paste, like butter, or a liquid, like milk, and used as a seasoning.

James Adair 1747...at the fall of the leaf, the woods are full of hiccory-nuts, acorns, chestnuts, and the like...*pg.281*
Col. James Smith 1755...while we remained here...went out to hunt chestnuts...*pg.140*
Benjamin Gilbert 1780...gathering hickory nuts...*pg.118*
John Tanner 1789...found some beech-nuts...*pg.11*
Mary Rowlandson 1676...I found six acorns and two chestnuts...*pg.37*
H.M. van den Bogaert 1634...they gave me a white hare [*cottontail*] to eat...it was cooked with chestnuts...*pg.21*
...also, we provided ourselves here with bread that we could take along on the journey. Some of it had nuts, chestnuts, dried blueberries and sunflower seeds baked in it...*pg.10*
Peter Kalm 1749...they make also many a delicious meal of the several kinds of walnuts, chestnuts...hazel nuts...*pg.533*
...they plant our common sunflower in their corn-fields, and mix the seeds of it into their sagamite or corn-soup...*pg.463*

Benjamin Gilbert 1780...they set about gathering their winter store of hickory nuts. From some of them they extracted an oil, which they eat with bread or meat, at their pleasure...*pg.147*

J. Heckewelder 1770...they pound the nuts in a block or mortar, pouring a little warm water on them, and gradually a little more as they become dry, until, at last, there is sufficient quantity of water, so that by stirring up the pounded nuts, the broken shells separate from the liquor, which from the pounded kernels assumes the appearance of milk. This being put into the kettle and mixed with the pottage gives it a rich and agreeable flavour...*pg.194*

Peter Kalm 1749...they likewise prepared a kind of liquor like milk by gathering a great number of hickory and black walnuts, dried and crushed them. Then took out the kernels, pounded them as fine as flour, and mixed this with water so that it looked like milk and was almost as sweet...*pg.269*

Thomas Hariot 1586...[*on nuts*] besides their eating of them after our ordinary maner, they breake them with stones and pound them in morters with water to make a milk which they use to put into some sorts of their spoonemeat; also among their sodden wheat [*cornmeal*], peaze, beanes and pompions [*pumpkins*] which maketh them have a farre more pleasant taste...

You will notice here, that "Fast Food" is not a new thing!

James Adair 1747...as he threw away his venison when he found himself pursued by the enemy, he was obliged to support nature with such herbs, roots, and nuts, as his sharp eyes with a running glance, directed him to snatch up in his course...*pg.317*

CHAPTER NINE

FRUITS & BERRIES

The Native cooks and travelers took full advantage of the many fruits and berries that grew wild throughout the country. Some of these were blueberries, blackberries, cranberries, red mulberries, gooseberries, strawberries, red and black raspberries, wild grapes, haws (hawthorn), crabapples, wild plums, and wild cherries. Besides being eaten fresh, they were added to breads, soups, and stews. They were also dried and stored for winter use, or combined with Jerk (the original "trail mix").

Peter Kalm 1749...they make also many a delicious meal of the several kinds of walnuts, chestnuts, mulberries, acimine [*papaw*], chinquapins [*nut*], hazel nuts, peaches [*European*], wild prunes [*plums*], grapes, whortleberries [*blueberries*] of several sorts, various kinds of medlars [*cucumber*], blackberries and other fruits and roots...*pg.533*
Dr. Knight 1782...there were wild gooseberries in abundance in the woods...*pg.14*
Col. James Smith 1755...I went down the run that we encamped on, in company with some squaws and boys to hunt plumbs, which we found in great plenty...*pg.133*
...this tour was at the time that the black haws [*hawthorn*] were ripe, and we were seldom out of sight of them; they were common here both in the bottoms and upland...*pg.137*
...there is a large quantity of wild apple, plumb, and red and black haw trees...*pg.139*
...hunting red haws, black haws, and hickory nuts...*pg.142*

Col. James Smith 1755...walnut, locust, mulberry, sugar-tree, red-haw, black-haw, wild-appletrees...*pg.163*
...I went...in order to gather cranberries...*pg.177*
...the land here...produces abundance of hurtle berries [*blueberries*]...*pg.183*
...about the sides of this pond there grew great abundance of cranberries, which the Indians gathered up...these berries were about as large as rifle bullets--of a bright red color--an agreeable sour, though rather too sour of themselves; but when mixed with sugar, had a very agreeable taste...*pg.165*
John M'Cullough 1756...we began to gather whortle-berries [*blueberries*], as they were very plenty...*pg.257*
Benjamin Gilbert 1780...as they took no game, they were under the necessity of eating wild cherries...*pg.144*
...on the journey he eat a land tortoise, some roots and wild cherries...*pg.145*
Robert Robison 1757...it was at the time of the plumbs being ripe...*pg.164*
O.M. Spencer 1792...I concluded to make my evening's meal on raspberries, which grew here in great abundance...*pg.55*
H.M. van den Bogaert 1634...and some dried strawberries...*pg.10*
J. Heckewelder 1770...they make an excellent preserve from the cranberry and crab-apple, to which, after it has been well stewed, they add a proper quantity of sugar or molasses [*maple sugar*]...*pg.194*
Peter Kalm 1749...Bilberries were likewise a very common dish among the Indians. They are called huckleberries by the English here, and belong to the various species of *Vaccinium* [*blueberries*]...the Indians plucked them in abundance every year, dried them either in the sunshine or by the fireside, and afterwards prepared them for eating in different manners...they offered me, whenever they designed to treat me well, fresh corn bread, baked in an oblong shape, mixed with dried huckleberries, which lay as close in it as the raisins in a plum pudding...*pg.262*

CHAPTER TEN

SPICES & SEASONINGS

Nature provided many unique sources of food seasoning. Maple sugar, and bear's oil (the fat of the bear, rendered down to a liquid), were the most common; followed by red pepper (cayenne and paprika), salt, garlic, mint, juniper berries, wild marjoram (oregano), wild ginger, and spicebush (wild allspice). Cornsilk was also dried and used to season and thicken broth.

Col. James Smith 1755...buckeye, sugar-tree [*maple*] and spicewood [*wild allspice*], are common...*pg.149*
...as sugar-trees were plenty and large here...*pg.147*
Benjamin Gilbert 1780...two men brought some Hommony, and sugar made from the sweet maple. The sap being boiled to a consistency, and is but a little inferior to the sugar imported from the Islands; of this provision, and an hedge-hog which they found, they made a more comfortable supper than they had enjoyed for many days...*pg.81*
...they staid about two months to gather their annual store of maple sugar, of which they made a considerable quantity...*pg.130*
O.M. Spencer 1792...we had had a remarkably fine season, and had been for several days employed, during which time we had collected sap sufficient to make, probably, a hundred weight of sugar...*pg.116*
John Tanner 1789...mukkuks [*birchbark containers*] of sugar, sacks of corn...*pg.9*
Alexander Henry 1760...we turned our attention to sugarmaking...*pg.95*

O.M. Spencer 1792...It was now near the close of February, when sharp, frosty nights, and days of warm sunshine, succeeding the extreme cold of winter, constituted what in early times in the west was called "sugar weather"; a season always improved by most families, who drew their year's supply from the sugar tree; and some made, besides quantities of sugar for sale. Taking our large brass kettle, with several smaller ones, some corn and beans for our sustenance, our bedding, and indeed all our household furniture and utensils...proceded four or five miles down the river [*to the trees*]...*pg.115*

Jemima Howe 1755...we came to a place where the Indians manufactured sugar, which they extracted from the maple trees...*pg.161*

Frances Noble 1755...he brought...a young fawn, and a basket of cranberries, and a lump of sap sugar...*pg.169*

Alexander Henry 1760...the fat of our bear was melted down and the oil filled six porcupine skins. A part of the meat was cut into strips and fired dried. Then it was put into the vessels containing the oil, where it remained in perfect preservation until the middle of summer...*pg.95*

Col. James Smith 1755...the squaws were then frying the last of their bears fat...one of these vessels would hold about four or five gallons; in these vessels it was what they carried their bears oil...*pg.148*

J. Heckewelder 1770...they are fond of dried venison, pounded in a mortar and dipped in bear's oil...*pg.196*

Col. James Smith 1755...the way that we commonly use our sugar while encamped, was by pitting it in bears fat until the fat was almost as sweet as the sugar itself, and in this we dipped our roasted venison...*pg.148*

...as we had brought with us on horse back, about two hundred weight of sugar, a large quantity of bears oil, etc...*pg.149*

...we then got some sugar, bears oil bottled up in bears gut, and some dry venison...*pg.150*

...gave him also sugar and bears oil, to eat with his venison...*pg.153*

Col. James Smith 1755...as the Indians on their return from their winter hunt, bring in with them large quantities of bears oil, sugar, dried venison...*pg.154*

...at this time homony, plentifully mixed with bears oil and sugar, or dried venison, bears oil and sugar, is what they offer to everyone who comes in any time of the day; and so they go on until their sugar, bears oil and venison is all gone, and then they have to eat homony by itself, without bread, salt, or anything else...*pg.155*

John M'Cullough 1756...we then moved to where they were settling a new town, called *Kseek-he'-oong*, that is, a place of salt, a place now well known by the name of salt licks...*pg.268*

...all the Indians...started off to the salt licks...*pg.279*

Peter Kalm 1749...had seen several salt springs in the country occupied by the native allies of the English and that the Indians prepared salt from them by the boiling method...the brine is boiled by the natives in copper utensils. Salt springs are found there in more than one place...*pg.609*

Col. James Smith 1755...we then moved to the buffaloe lick, where we killed several buffaloe, and in their small brass kettles they made about half a bushel of salt...*pg.134*

Peter Kalm 1749...a kind of seed was called...Capsicum [*red pepper*]. This is used very commonly here to improve the flavor of food. It is used very much as pepper is...*pg.611*

Dr. Knight 1782...when my food sat heavy on my stomach, I used to eat a little wild ginger which put all to right...*pg.15* [*natural antacid!*]

Susanna Johnson 1754...broth was made for me and my child, which was rendered almost a luxury by the seasoning of roots...*pg.61*

...the marrow bones were pounded for a soup; and every root, both sweet and bitter, that the woods afforded, was thrown in to give it a flavor...*pg.61*

CHAPTER ELEVEN

BEVERAGES

Although there is very little primary source documentation on beverages, over the years there have been other studies done on this subject. Besides water, teas were made from various barks, roots, and berries, such as sassafras, wild allspice, red sumac berries, cranberries, and blueberries. The broth from soup was also a common beverage. The juice from corn stalks and cane stalks was used, but usually as a temporary substitute for water.

O.M. Spencer 1792...I had now to make fires, carry water both for cooking and drinking...*pg.108*
J. Heckewelder 1770...a large kettle of tea had been made by some of the good women, who invited all to come and take their share of it...*pg.197*
Capt. Spencer Records 1784...spice-wood tea [*wild allspice or sassafras*]...*pg.64*
G.H. Loskiel 1794...the common drink of the Indians at their meals is nothing but the broth of the meat they have boiled, or spring water. [*They also*] prepare a kind of liquor of dried bilberries [*blueberries*], sugar and water, the taste of which is very agreeable to them...
Nehemiah How 1745...they boiled a good mess of it [*soup*]. I drank of the broth, eat of the meat and corn, and was wonderfully refreshed...*pg.128*
Mary Rowlandson 1676...they boiled an old horse's leg which they had got, and so we drank of the broth...*pg.31*

Elizabeth Hanson 1724...[*on making baby formula*] take the kernels of walnuts, clean them and beat them with a little water, which I did and when I had done so, the water looked like milk; then she advised me to add to this water a little of the finest of Indian corn meal, and boil it a little together...*pg.121*

Mrs. Frances Scott 1785...she had no other food to subsist upon but what she derived from chewing and swallowing the juice of young cane stalks, sassafras leaves, and some other plants of which she knew not the names...*pg.341*

Father Lafitau 1724...for the stem of the maize [*corn*] when it is full of juice is filled with a honeyed water, very healthy and very refreshing...*pg.93*

CHAPTER TWELVE

EUROPEAN GOODS

I have included this chapter on European introduced goods, because some foods were quickly adapted and cultivated by the Native people. Many of these became a part of their everyday diet. Some, like sweet potatoes and lima beans, originally from South America, were first taken to Europe and then brought back, by the Europeans, to North America. The other introduced goods were apples, peaches, watermelon, peas, turnips, cabbage, carrots, potatoes, wheat, honey, and several herbs, such as dill, sage, bay leaf, and parsley. Beef, pork, and chicken became common; plus milk, butter, and sugar. I have also included chocolate in this section. Although "cacao" is also indigenous to the Americas, and widely consumed since ancient times, the sweet chocolate that we are familiar with was unknown in Eastern North America. Not until its reintroduction by the Europeans, in its new form, did it become popular.

Mrs. McCoy 1747...the Indians then collected...the apples of the only tree which bore in town...*pg.144*
...the apples they had gathered they saved for her, giving her one every day...*pg.145*
Mary Jemison 1755...[*the army*] destroyed our fruit-trees...*pg.123*
John M'Cullough 1756...bread, meat, watermelons...*pg.289*
...watermelon, or cucumber patches...*pg.269*
...the plundering of a watermelon patch...*pg.272*
Susanna Johnson 1754...the savages...gave us a loaf of bread, some raisins, and apples which they had taken from the house...*pg.57*

Zadock Steele 1780...we then prepared our camp, built a fire, and, having procured some turnips, kept continually roasting them successively during the night...eating cold meat with roasted turnips till the approach of day...*pg.140*

Peter Kalm 1749...the Indians were very fond of turnips, and called them sometimes *Hopniss*, sometimes *Katniss*...*pg.268* [*these are the same names for groundnuts and arrowhead roots, because of a similar appearance*].

Benjamin Gilbert 1780...having in addition to their usual bill of fare, plenty of turnips and potatoes, which had remained in the ground...*pg.79*

Zadock Steele 1780...the Indians...had secreted a number of bags of fine flour which they brought with them from Canada, and now regained. This greatly replenished their stores, and afforded a full supply of wholesome bread. The manner of making their bread is curious, and exhibits useful instruction to those who may be called to make their bread in the wilderness without enjoying the privilege of household furniture. They took their dough, wound it around a stick in the form of a screw, stuck it into the ground by the fire, and thus baked their bread...*pg.107*

...we had prepared some food for our sustenance on the way by taking a quantity of flour and mixing it with melted butter, which we put into a small bag made for the purpose. We also had a little salt pork and bread, together with some parched corn and black pepper...*pg.129*

...none of our provisions remained fit to carry with us except a little parched corn, which was in a small, wooden bottle, some salt pork, and our buttered flour, which we found to be waterproof...*pg.130*

Benjamin Gilbert 1780...they divided some bread, which they had brought, into small pieces...*pg.83*

Mary Rowlandson 1676...he gave me a pancake about as big as two fingers; it was made of parched wheat, beaten and fried in bear's grease, but I thought I never tasted pleasanter meat in my life...*pg.34*

Col. James Smith 1755...the principal grain that the French raised in these fields was spring wheat and peas...*pg.183*

Father Lafitau 1724...the wheat brought by the French to America is certainly much more recent there than maize. The Indians, however, give the same name to both in their language...*pg.50*

Mary Jemison 1755...[*on food storage*] corn...together with beans, sugar, and honey, so carefully buried that it was completely dry, and as good as when they left it...*pg.77*

Nehemiah How 1745...some of the Indians went and got a plenty of bread and beef, which they put into the canoes...*pg.131*

...the Indians who were killing cattle came to us, laden with beef...we roasted the meat they had got...*pg.127*

Mary Rowlandson 1676...I boiled my peas and beef together...*pg.34*

...gave me a piece of fresh pork, and a little salt with it, and lent me her frying pan to fry it...*pg.50*

...would give me some pork and ground-nuts...*pg.49*

Robert Eastburn 1756...on my return, the Indians perceiving that I was unwell, and could not eat their coarse food, ordered some chocolate, which they had brought from the Carrying Place, to be boiled for me, and seeing me eat that, appeared pleased...*pg.21*

Capt. Spencer Records 1784...a great many cakes of chocolate...*pg.77*

Charles Johnston 1790...the boats were taken to the shore and their contents landed. The chiefs distributed the plunder among their followers. Flour, sugar and chocolate formed a part if it. They probably believed I understood the subject of making flour into bread better than they did, and that chore was assigned to me...I began by baking a number of loaves in the ashes. There was more dough than the fire would contain and I decided to make the remainder into small dumplings and boil them in a kettle of chocolate then on the fire. All savages are particularly fond of sweet things. To gratify this taste, they had mixed a large portion of sugar with the chocolate, and this made the dumplings quite sweet. The Indians were so delighted with this new delicious dish that they appeared to consider me a very clever fellow as a cook, and gave me that job...*pg.193* [*yum!*]

RECIPES

TRADITIONAL & MODERN

This section contains both traditional recipes and preparation methods, as well as, the modern adaptations. For those of you who want to prepare things in a historically accurate fashion, you will find open fire cooking and sun drying. I firmly believe in doing things in a traditional manner, it helps us to understand where we came from and how we got here. It also teaches us to respect and appreciate what our ancestors had to do to survive.
Sometimes, the fast pace of modern life does not allow us time to do things in a totally authentic way. If you are interested in taking a few short-cuts, with the same results, I have included those too. I think that both ways are good. The important thing is that you, at least, try. Don't be afraid to experiment!

* Some recipes will not have actual quantities listed since there are so many variables, but most will serve two to four people.

Historical "trade goods" trivia: What was the difference between a *pot* and a *kettle*?
A *pot* was bulbous, and narrowed near the top before flaring out, and usually had a lid.
A *kettle* had straighter sides that widened at the top, and generally had no lid.

Helpful Hints

* SOME PLANTS CAN BE TOXIC AT CERTAIN TIMES OF THE YEAR. **PLEASE**, MAKE SURE YOU CORRECTLY IDENTIFY EACH BEFORE COOKING OR EATING!

* European introduced goods in any recipe will be noted separately as, *optional*.

* In all of the recipes calling for dried beans; if using traditionally, there are two ways to prepare for cooking. You must soak in water overnight, *or* quick soak by boiling in water for 2 minutes, remove from heat, cover and let stand for 1 hour. This must be drained and fresh water added to cook. For the modern method, you may use canned or frozen products, remembering that these will only take 1/3 the cooking time.

* Try to get fresh produce from your own garden or farm market. Produce that has not been refrigerated will keep much longer than what you get in the grocery store. Do not wash vegetables until just before use. Contrary to popular belief the *watering* at the stores does not keep things fresher. Moisture only causes faster deterioration. However, once refrigerated it must stay that way.

* To Sun dry fresh produce: Lay or hang pieces in the sun, turning frequently until completely dry. This can take from a few days to weeks, depending on what the weather is like, and what you are drying. (Meat and Fish *should not* be dried this way).

* To Oven dry meat or produce: Set the oven on the lowest heat possible, turning pieces occasionally until completely dry. This can take from 12 hours to overnight, depending on what and how much you are drying.

* Using a Dehydrator to dry meat or produce: Since all are different, follow the manufacturers' instructions. Drying can take from 3 hours to 12 hours, depending on what you are drying and the volume.

* Many old recipes call for bear oil. Since this is quite hard to come by for most people, you may substitute oil, lard, or bacon grease in any of the recipes. It's not the same taste; but it will do.

* *Meat* can be venison, elk, buffalo, or bear. Beef may be substituted for these in any of the recipes.

* Brown or white sugar may be substituted for the Maple Sugar.

MEAT

ROASTING MEAT

The most common method of cooking meat, was simply to put it on a stick over or near the fire, and turning it frequently, roast it until it was done. This could be done with large pieces, such as a hind quarter or rump roast, or smaller individual pieces. To roast the larger can take from 2 to 6 hours; smaller pieces may only take minutes. For a more elaborate meal we reach for the kettle...

VENISON ROAST

2 LB. VENISON ROAST
2 T. OIL OR LARD
2 ONIONS, CUBED
2 CLOVES GARLIC, MINCED

4 C. WATER
optional:
4 CARROTS, SLICED
4 POTATOES, CUBED

In large pot, brown venison in hot oil. Add onions, garlic and water. Cover and cook for 30 minutes. Add *carrots and cook 30 more minutes. Add *potatoes and continue cooking, covered, for 30 minutes more, or until meat is done and vegetables are tender, adding water if necessary. Serves 2-3.

VENISON & CORN SOUP

2 T. OIL OR LARD
1 LARGE ONION, CHOPPED
1 CLOVE GARLIC, MINCED
1 LB. VENISON, CUBED

6 C. WATER
4 C. CORN, FRESH
1 t. CAYENNE PEPPER
SALT, TO TASTE

In large pot, sauté onions and garlic in hot oil, until onions are transparent. Add venison and water. Simmer, covered, over medium heat for 1 hour, or until meat is tender. Add corn and cayenne pepper. Simmer for 10 minutes, or until corn is tender. Salt to taste, if desired. Serve hot. Serves 4.

MEAT

ELK STEW

1 LB. ELK MEAT, CUBED
2 T. OIL OR LARD
3 C. WATER
1 MEDIUM ONION, CHOPPED
1 BAY LEAF, *optional*

1/2 t. SALT
2 *POTATOES, CUBED
2 YELLOW SQUASH, CUBED
2 T. CORNMEAL + 1/4 C. WATER

In large pot, brown meat in hot oil. Add water, onion, *bay leaf, and salt. Cover and simmer over medium heat for 1 hour. Add *potatoes and squash. Cook 20 minutes more, or until vegetables are tender. Combine cornmeal and water. Slowly stir enough into simmering stew to thicken. Serve hot. Serves 2-3.

(Dried cornsilk could also be used as a thickener. See *SPICES & SEASONINGS*.)

BUFFALO & WILD RICE

1/2 LB. BUFFALO, CUBED
1 T. OIL OR LARD
3 GREEN ONIONS, SLICED
3 TO 4 C. WATER

1 t. SAGE, *optional*
1 C. WILD RICE
1/4 t. SALT & *PEPPER
1/2 C. HAZELNUTS, CHOPPED

In large pot, brown meat and onions in hot oil. Remove, and set aside. Bring water to a boil, add wild rice, meat, and onions. Cover, cook over low heat for 30 minutes, or until half the water is absorbed. Add *sage, salt, and *pepper. Cover, continue cooking until rice is tender and meat is done. Stir in hazelnuts during last 10 minutes, if desired. Serves 3-4.

MEAT

MEAT & BERRY SOUP

1 1/2 LBS. VENISON, CUBED
2 T. OIL OR LARD
4 C. MEAT BROTH OR WATER
1 C. GREEN ONION, SLICED
1 C. BLACKBERRIES,
OR BLUEBERRIES
1 T. MAPLE SUGAR
SALT, TO TASTE

In large pot, brown meat in hot oil. Add broth, onions, berries, and maple sugar. Simmer over medium heat for 1 hour, or until meat is tender. Season with salt, if desired. Serves 4.

(Blackberries can be fresh or frozen.)

DEER LIVER & ONIONS

1 LB. LIVER
2 T. OIL OR LARD + 1/4 C.
1 LARGE ONION, SLICED
1/2 C. CORNMEAL
optional:
1/2 t. SAGE

Slice liver 1/2 inch thick. Combine cornmeal and *sage. Coat liver slices with cornmeal mixture. In heavy pan, heat oil until melted. Add onions and sauté until tender. Remove, keep warm. Heat 1/4 cup oil in same pan. Add liver. Fry over medium heat until liver is browned, 2 to 3 minutes on each side. Return onions to pan to heat through. Serve hot. Serves 4.

(Another option is to use *bacon in place of the oil. Fry bacon until crispy, remove and set aside. Fry onions, then liver, in bacon grease.)

MEAT

ROAST RABBIT

1 2 1/2 to 3 LB. RABBIT,
   WHOLE OR CUT IN PIECES
SALT, (PEPPER, *optional*)

CAYENNE PEPPER,
OR PAPRIKA

Sprinkle salt, *pepper, cayenne or paprika on rabbit. Put on skewer or stick over fire. Roast, turning often, until cooked through; or broil in oven on medium-high heat for 20 minutes, turn, broil 20 minutes more. Serve hot. Serves 2.

RABBIT & WILD RICE

1 2 1/2 to 3 LB. RABBIT,
      CUT IN PIECES
2-3 T. OIL OR LARD
SALT, (PEPPER, *optional*)
CAYENNE PEPPER,
      OR PAPRIKA

2 1/2 C. WATER
1 MEDIUM ONION,
      CHOPPED
2 CLOVES GARLIC,
      MINCED
1 C. WILD RICE

Combine salt, *pepper, cayenne or paprika. Coat rabbit pieces with mixture. Heat oil in large pot. Brown rabbit pieces on both sides. Add water, onions and garlic. Simmer, covered, over medium-high heat for 1 hour. Add wild rice and cook, covered for 45 minutes more, or until rice is tender and water is absorbed. Add more water as needed, watching carefully so it does not boil over. Serve hot. Serves 2-3.

(You could also add hazelnuts or chestnuts during the last 15 minutes of cooking, if desired. Green onions could also be substituted for the regular onion.)

JERK

MAKING JERK

The traditional method of making Jerk: Cut the meat (venison, buffalo, etc.) into thin even slices. It is usually not seasoned, so that it can be stored longer. Build a hot, long burning fire. When you have a good bed of coals, place a grate or sticks over the fire. Lay the slices on these, over the coals. Keep fire low and constant. Turn pieces occasionally to ensure even drying. This can take 8 to 12 hours, depending on the weather, the fire, and the amount of meat you are jerking. This gives the meat a naturally smoky flavor.

The modern oven method, is to again cut the meat into thin even slices. Season, if desired, with salt, cayenne, sugar, *liquid smoke, or a marinade, etc. Place strips on oven rack. Do not overlap. Place aluminum foil or baking sheet underneath rack to catch drippings. Set oven temperature to 140°F to 160°F (60°C to 70°C) for the first 8 to 10 hours. Then lower to 130°F (55°C) until dry. If your oven settings are not this low, just use the lowest heat setting you have, and leave the oven door slightly open. You may turn pieces occasionally while drying, if desired. When completely dry, jerk should crack when bent, but not break. There should be no signs of moisture.

Using a dehydrator can be time-saving, as well as cost efficient. If you plan to use a large quantity of dried foods (for *trekking*, etc.) I would highly recommend investing in one. There are many different models, in all price ranges available today. Each model has its own temperature settings, and you should follow the manufacturers' directions. Generally, you will prepare the meat as already mentioned. Lay the strips onto the drying trays. The heat setting will be around 145°F (63°C). You will not need to turn the pieces as they are drying. The meat will be dry in 4 to 6 hours, depending on the dehydrator, and the quantity being made.

* 1 lb. of fresh meat will yield approximately 1/4 lb. of Jerk.

JERK

MODERN JERK MARINADE

WATER + LIQUID SMOKE + SPICES OF YOUR CHOICE
(garlic, dill, pepper, cayenne, etc.)

Soak meat overnight in marinade. Remove and drain. Place on drying racks in oven or dehydrator. Dry.
(For drying directions, see *Making Jerk*.)

JERK SOUP

1/2 LB. JERK, BREAK IN PIECES
1 C. HOMINY, DRIED
WATER, TO COVER
1 SMALL ONION, CHOPPED
2 SUMMER SQUASH, SLICED
SALT, TO TASTE

In large pot, combine hominy, jerk, onion, and enough water to cover. Bring to a boil. Reduce heat, and simmer, covered, for 1 to 1 1/2 hours, or until hominy and jerk are tender. Add squash, and salt to taste. Cook 20 minutes more, until squash is tender. Serve hot. Serves 2-3.

(Jerusalem artichokes may also be added with the squash, if desired. If Jerk is already seasoned, extra salt may not be needed.)

JERK & BEANS

1/2 LB. DRIED BEANS (ABOUT 1 C.), PRESOAKED, DRAINED
3 C. WATER
1 SMALL ONION, CHOPPED
JERK, BREAK IN PIECES

In large pot, combine all ingredients. Cook over medium heat for 1 to 1 1/2 hours, or until beans are tender. Serve hot. Serves 2.

FISH

ROAST FISH

Place cleaned whole fish near hot coals, or hang on a stick over low fire. Turn occasionally until cooked through and fish flakes easily. If fish is large use small sticks to hold body open. You may also lightly season with salt or cayenne pepper, if desired.

ROASTED STUFFED FISH

This works best with a good sized fish, like large-mouth bass or trout. Rub inside of fish with salt. Stuff with cooked wild rice, onion, and garlic. You can also use any finely chopped vegetables. Close opening with wood skewers, strips of corn husks, or whatever is handy. Rub outside of fish with oil or grease. Place near hot coals or on grate over coals. Roast for 1 hour, turning occasionally. Fish is done when it flakes easily.

BOILED FISH

Clean fish, removing head and tail. Put in kettle with water just to cover. Boil until tender and flakes easily. Remove to bowl. Salt to taste. Serve hot.

BOILED FISH & *POTATOES

8 SMALL WHOLE *POTATOES
WATER, TO COVER
8 SMALL WHOLE ONIONS

2-3 T. SALT
8 FISH CHUNKS
***optional:** 2 BAY LEAVES*

In large pot, place *potatoes in enough water to cover. Bring to a boil. Add salt and onions. Cook for 20 minutes. Add fish chunks and *bay leaves. Cover and boil gently for 10-15 minutes, or until potatoes are tender and fish flakes easily. Drain. Serve.   Serves 4.

FISH

FISH SOUP

Boil fish in quantity of water. When cooked through, add cornmeal to thicken. Season as desired. Serve hot.

FISH & CORN SOUP

1 C. ONION, CHOPPED	1 t. SALT
2 T. OIL OR LARD	1 LB. FISH CHUNKS
1 C. FRESH BEANS	2 T. CORNMEAL
4 C. WATER	*optional:*
1 C. FRESH CORN	2 T. PARSLEY

In large pot, sauté onion in hot oil until soft. Add beans, water, corn, salt, and fish. Cover and simmer for 20 minutes, stirring occasionally, until beans and corn are tender and fish is cooked. Stir in cornmeal to thicken. Add *parsley. Stir well.   Serves 4.

DRIED & SMOKED FISH

Some traditional ways of drying and smoking fish, were to rub the cleaned fish with salt, and dry over an open fire, slowly. Or open the fish flat with skewers and place on sticks in front of the fire to dry. Or hang the fish in the rafters of the longhouse, above the fire pits in the smoke, until they were completely dry.

A modern method of drying fish (Fish Jerk) is to cut the fish into thin strips. Soak these for 30 minutes in 1 quart of cold water plus 1/2 cup of salt. Rinse in fresh water. Place on large tray. Generously sprinkle with salt, *pepper, and *liquid smoke. Place the strips in an airtight glass or plastic container. Refrigerate 4-8 hours. Dry in the oven or dehydrator at 140°F to 160°F (60°C to 70°C) for 12-14 hours, or until completely dry.

FOWL

ANOTHER "BRUNSWICK" STEW

(This is reputed to be one of the first meals introduced to the Jamestown settlers by the Native people.)

1 3 1/2 to 4 LB. RABBIT (OR *CHICKEN), CUT IN PIECES
3 T. OIL OR LARD
SALT, CAYENNE OR PAPRIKA (PEPPER, *optional)
6 C. BROTH OR WATER
1 LARGE ONION, CHOPPED
1 CLOVE GARLIC, MINCED
3 POTATOES, CUBED, *optional
2 C. DRIED KIDNEY BEANS, SOAKED, DRAINED
2 C. FRESH CORN (OR FROZEN)
1 C. FRESH GREEN BEANS
1/2 t. DRIED OREGANO
1 BAY LEAF, *optional
FRESH PARSLEY, MINCED, *optional

Season rabbit or *chicken pieces with salt, *pepper, cayenne or paprika. In large kettle, brown rabbit in hot oil. Add broth, and simmer for 15 minutes. Add remaining ingredients. Simmer for 1 hour, or until meat and vegetables are tender. Stir in fresh *parsley. Serve hot.   Serves 4.

TURKEY & CORN STEW

1 1/2 to 2 LBS. TURKEY, CUT IN PIECES   2 1/2 C. WATER
2 T. OIL OR LARD   *optional:
1 C. ONION, CHOPPED   1/4 t. PEPPER
1 C. FRESH CORN (OR FROZEN)   FRESH PARSLEY

In large pot, brown turkey pieces in hot oil. Add water, onions, *pepper and *parsley. Simmer, covered, over low heat for 45 minutes. Add corn and continue cooking for 20 minutes more, or until turkey is cooked through.   Serves 4.

CORN

ROAST CORN

One of the easiest (and tastiest) ways that corn was served, were whole roasted ears. After picking the corn, husks were pulled back, but not removed. The cornsilk was taken off and saved (see *SPICES & SEASONINGS*), and the husks were pulled back up around the ears. Sometimes they were tied closed by using strips of husk, or just twisted closed. The corn was then soaked in water (for about 20 minutes). The cobs were placed on hot coals, and turned frequently (for about 40 minutes). The husks would turn black, but they kept the steam inside. When done, the husks were pulled back and the corn was eaten off the cob. Sometimes dipped in bear oil as extra flavoring.

CORN & DUCK STEW

1 C. DUCK, PIECES	3 t. MAPLE SUGAR
1 T. OIL OR LARD	SALT, TO TASTE
1 ONION, CHOPPED	1/2 C. *MUSHROOMS
4 C. BOILING WATER	1/4 C. HAZELNUTS,
1 C. CORN, DRIED	CHOPPED

In large kettle, brown duck pieces in hot oil. Add remaining ingredients, except hazelnuts. Simmer over medium heat, 1 to 1 1/2 hours, or until duck is cooked through and corn is tender. Stir in hazelnuts during last 25 minutes. Serve hot.   Serves 4.

CORN & BEANS

From the Narraganset word *"msickquatash"*, we are all familiar with *succotash*, or corn and beans. Using equal amounts of dried corn and cranberry beans (limas were rare in the 17th century), these were soaked, and then boiled together until tender. Seasoned with maple sugar or salt, this was common fare.

HOMINY

MAKING HOMINY

2 QUARTS DRY, RIPE FIELD CORN
2 C. HARD WOOD ASHES

Traditionally everything was thrown into the pot. Today we put the ashes into a cheese cloth bag, tie it and place into a large kettle with the corn. Cover with warm water and let stand overnight. The next day, boil until the hulls come off. Wash well in several changes of water, rubbing the corn between your hands. This is now ready to dry, or pound into flour, or cook as it is.
To cook, place corn into fresh cold water and bring to a boil. Cook until the corn is tender. This will take 3-4 hours. Serve with maple sugar. This was common for breakfast.

DRIED HOMINY

1 C. DRIED HOMINY   1 t. SALT   WATER, TO COVER

In medium sized pot, bring water, hominy, and salt to a boil. Reduce heat and simmer, covered, for 1 1/2 hours, or until hominy is tender. Watch carefully so that it does not boil over. Serve with maple sugar, or (honey, *optional*).   Serves 3-4.

HOMINY SOUP

Traditional hominy soup was simply a combination of dried hominy, boiled with whatever meat, beans, vegetables, nuts, or berries were available. Seasoned with maple sugar or bear oil, this made a hearty meal.

HOMINY

HOMINY & SUNFLOWER SOUP

2/3 C. DRIED HOMINY
1 C. DRIED BEANS, SOAKED
1 C. SUNFLOWER SEEDS,
        SHELLED

1 ONION, CHOPPED
1 CLOVE GARLIC,
        MINCED
SALT, TO TASTE

In large pot, combine hominy and beans with enough water to cover. Bring to a boil. Reduce heat, simmer covered for 2 1/2 hours, or until tender. Watch carefully to avoid boil over. Add water as needed. Add sunflower seeds, onion, and garlic, continue cooking for 30 minutes more. Add salt to taste. Serves 4.

(The sunflower seeds will surprise you. Not only will they thicken the broth, it will make the broth taste like chicken!)

NUT BUTTER HOMINY

2/3 C. DRIED HOMINY
WATER, TO COVER

2 T. NUT BUTTER
1 T. MAPLE SUGAR

In large pot, combine hominy and water. Bring to a boil. Reduce heat, and simmer, covered, over low heat for 1 1/2 hours, or until hominy is tender. Adding water if needed. Add nut butter and maple sugar. Stir well. Serve hot.   Serves 2-3.

(The recipe for nut butter can be found under *NUTS & SEEDS*.)

Hominy can be used in any corn recipe. The flavor is heartier, and the texture makes it more filling than fresh corn. Canned hominy tastes **nothing** like real dried hominy! Use canned if you must, but I would not recommend it.

PARCHED CORN

PARCHED CORN

Next to meat, probably *the* most important food item consumed was parched corn; corn that was dried and roasted. Corn prepared in this manner had many benefits. It could be preserved almost indefinitely. Surviving evidence is still being found at archeological sites. It was light and easy to carry while traveling, and almost *weather-proof*. It was nourishing, as well as, filling. On the trail, a handful of parched corn, pounded into a meal, and some water was all one would need to feel satisfied. Parched corn was also an important part of the winter food supply.

MAKING PARCHED CORN

Traditional: Take fresh ears of ripe field, or flint corn and pull back the husks, but do not remove. Remove the cornsilk. Tie or braid the husks together, and hang the corn in a warm, dry place until completely dry. This usually takes a few weeks. Then remove the kernels from the cob. Place the kernels, a handful at a time, in a heavy pan and brown over an open fire. Stirring often so they will not burn. When parched, the hard dry kernels will turn golden brown, and puff up slightly. They will be crunchy, but easy to chew. Maple sugar, and sometimes salt, were often mixed with the parched corn for added flavor.
Modern: Use fresh or frozen kernels of corn. If oven drying, place a single layer on an ungreased baking sheet. Dry at 150°F(65°C) for about 8 hours, or until completely dry. Stir occasionally. If you are using a dehydrator, it will take about 4 hours to dry.
When corn is totally dry, brown a handful at a time, in a heavy skillet. You may use a *small* amount of oil or grease for extra flavor, if desired. Watch carefully, stirring often. This can burn very quickly. With no added oil, parched corn can last for months.

POPCORN

YES, POPCORN

Popcorn was another favorite Native food. Not consumed quite like we do today, it was usually pounded into a type of flour. The ears of corn were sometimes placed near the fire and the whole cob popped, or the kernels were removed and popped in a kettle over the fire. The freshly popped kernels were then put into a mortar and pounded, or ground into coarse meal, and sifted. This was then mixed with maple sugar and eaten like parched corn, or added to soups and stews.

POPCORN SOUP

3-4 C. POPPED POPCORN
4 C. WATER OR BROTH
1/2 LB. STEW MEAT
1/2 C. ONION, CHOPPED
SALT, TO TASTE
2 C. VEGETABLES, CHOPPED

Pound or ground popcorn into a meal, and sift. In large pot, combine all ingredients. Cook over medium heat for 1 hour, or until meat is tender. Season to taste. Serve hot. Serves 2-3.

(To make a sweet soup: omit the onion and salt. Add maple sugar to taste.)

POPCORN MUSH

POPCORN, POUNDED, SIFTED
BOILING WATER
MAPLE SUGAR, OR
*optional: HONEY

In large bowl, slowly add boiling water to popcorn meal, until it thickens to desired consistency. Serve hot with maple sugar.

BREAD

CORN BREAD

Bread made of corn has been a staple of the Native American diet since prehistoric times. It has been made many different ways, with many different ingredients, but it always remains basically the same; corn and water. Fresh corn, dried cornmeal, hominy, and hominy meal were used. Added to this were beans, nuts, berries, pumpkin, etc. The bread was baked, boiled, or made into dumplings.

ASH CAKES

2 C. CORNMEAL   1 t. SALT, IF DESIRED
HOT OR BOILING WATER

In bowl, combine cornmeal and salt. Slowly add hot water to make a stiff dough. Shape into small cakes and place in or near hot ashes. Bake until lightly browned on both sides.   Makes 6.

BOILED CORN BREAD

2 C. CORNMEAL   BOILING WATER

In bowl, combine cornmeal and enough boiling water to make a stiff paste. Shape into balls or cakes. Keep hands moistened with cold water. Drop bread into kettle of boiling water. Cook for 30 minutes, or until cakes tend to float.   Makes 6-8.

The additions to both if these basic breads are endless. Before cooking, just stir in any of the following: cooked meat, cooked beans, fresh or dried squash, cooked pumpkin or sweet potatoes, fresh or dried berries, nuts, maple sugar...(see what I mean?)
It all tastes good!

BREAD

CRANBERRY DUMPLINGS

1 1/2 C. CORNMEAL
1/2 C. CRANBERRIES, CHOPPED
BOILING WATER
2 T. MAPLE SUGAR, OR
optional: HONEY

In large bowl, combine cornmeal, cranberries, and sugar or *honey. Slowly stir in boiling water to make a stiff paste. Shape into small cakes or balls. Drop into boiling water, or onto boiling stew. Cook 30 minutes.   Makes 6-8.

(Any berry can be substituted for the cranberries.)

CORN, PUMPKIN & BERRY CAKES

2 1/2 C. CORNMEAL
1/2 C. BLACKBERRIES
BOILING WATER
1 C. PUMPKIN, SLICED
2 T. MAPLE SUGAR, OR
optional: HONEY

In large bowl, combine cornmeal and boiling water. In medium sized pot, boil pumpkin down to a thin mush. Add to cornmeal mixture. Stir in blackberries and maple sugar. Shape into small cakes and drop into boiling water. Cook 40 minutes, or until cakes float. These can also be baked in hot ashes instead of boiled.   Makes 10 cakes.

HOMINY PANCAKES

2 C. HOMINY MEAL
2 T. OIL OR LARD
2 t. SALT
HOT WATER

In large bowl, combine hominy meal, oil, and salt. Add enough hot water to make a thick batter. Pour onto a hot griddle and fry until brown. Serve with maple syrup or (honey, *optional*).

LEAF BREAD

LEAF BREAD

Even if this bread did not taste good (which it does), the concept is quite interesting, and it is fun to make.
The basic cornmeal, or hominy meal mixture, with or without extra ingredients, was wrapped up in the green leaves of the corn plant. Tied closed with strips of the husk. These were then dropped into boiling water and cooked.
Mexican tamales are basically the same thing.
Fresh or "green" corn, pounded to a paste, was also cooked this way.

LEAF BREAD WITH MEAT

1 C. HOMINY MEAL
BOILING WATER
CORN HUSKS, GREEN OR DRIED
1 t. ONION, CHOPPED
1 C. COOKED MEAT, SHREDDED
1 t. SALT
1/8 t. CAYENNE PEPPER

If using dried corn husks, soak in hot water before using.
In bowl, combine cooked meat, onion, salt, and cayenne. Set aside. In large bowl, combine hominy meal with boiling water, to form a thick paste. Spread a spoonful of the paste onto husks. Put a spoonful of the meat mixture in the center. Roll up, fold ends, and tie closed using strips of husk. Place into pot of boiling water. Boil for 20 minutes. Remove husks and serve.

LEAF NUT BREAD

1 C. HOMINY MEAL   BOILING WATER   1 C. NUTS, CHOPPED

Combine meal and water. Stir in nuts. Wrap dough in corn husks, and drop into boiling water. Boil for 15-20 minutes. Remove husks and serve.

LEAF BREAD

GREEN CORN BREAD

In numerous 17th and 18th century narratives there are many references to *green* corn. This is what the Natives called fresh corn, in the milk stage. The corn kernels were scraped off the cobs and put into a mortar. Adding a little water at a time, this was pounded into a paste. The paste was wrapped in corn husks, and boiled or baked in hot ashes. Very often other things were added to this mixture; nuts, berries, etc.

PUMPKIN BREAD

PUMPKIN OR SQUASH, COOKED
1/2 C. CORNMEAL
1/4 t. ALLSPICE
OIL OR LARD

1 t. SALT
1/2 C. CHOPPED NUTS, OR BERRIES

Remove pulp from pumpkin, or peel squash, and place in large bowl. Mash. Stir in cornmeal, allspice, and salt, to make a dough. Add water if too dry. Stir in chopped nuts or berries, if desired. Heat oil on griddle. Drop spoonfuls of dough onto hot griddle. Brown on both sides. Serve hot. You may also shape into cakes and bake in hot ashes, or wrap in green corn leaves and boil until done. Serve hot.   Makes 10-12.

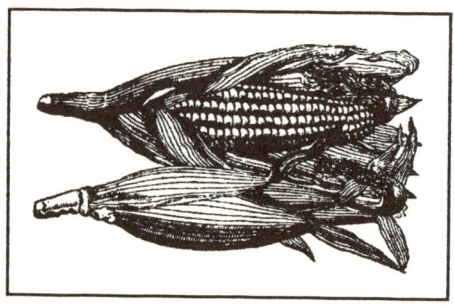

BEANS

BEANS

Beans were used fresh or dried, shelled or in the pod. The different types of beans were used interchangeably in any meal. The exception to this being the pod type green or "string" bean, which was not used in the making of bread. Beans were usually boiled alone, or added to other foods.

CRANBERRY BEANS & CORN

Fresh shelled cranberry beans, or cooked dried beans, are mixed with an equal amount of fresh green corn. Boil together about 15-20 minutes or until corn is tender. Cooked meat may be added for extra flavor. Season with bear oil or salt, if desired.

GREEN BEANS & JERK

1/2 LB. FRESH GREEN BEANS
JERK, BROKEN IN PIECES

Place beans and jerk in pot, cover with water. Simmer until tender, about 15-20 minutes. Drain. Season with salt, if desired. Serve hot.

Serves 2.

DRIED BEAN SOUP

Pound dry beans in a mortar. Soak in cold water for 8 hours. Boil with pieces of meat or jerk until tender. Season with maple sugar or salt, to taste. Serve hot.

BEANS

BEANS & SQUASH

1 C. DRIED BEANS, COOKED
1 T. OIL OR LARD
1 SMALL ONION, SLICED,
1 CLOVE GARLIC, MINCED SLICED
1/2 t. WILD MARJORAM (OREGANO)
2 MEDIUM ZUCCHINI,
2 YELLOW SQUASH, SLICED
1/4 t. SALT
PINCH OF CAYENNE

In large pot, cook onions and garlic in hot oil until tender. Stir in remaining ingredients. Heat to boiling; reduce heat. Cover and simmer 10-15 minutes, or until vegetables are tender.   Serves 4.

SWEET BEAN SOUP

Cook fresh shelled beans until tender. Add maple sugar to taste.

MEAT, SQUASH & BEAN SOUP

1 LB. MEAT, CUT IN CHUNKS
2 C. WATER
1 C. DRIED KIDNEY BEANS, SOAKED OVERNIGHT
1/8 t. GINGER
1/8 t. CAYENNE
1 t. SALT
1 C. SUMMER SQUASH, SLICED

In large pot, heat meat, water, beans, ginger, and cayenne to boiling. Reduce heat. Simmer, covered, for 2 hours or until meat and beans are tender. Stir in squash and salt. Simmer for 15-20 minutes, until squash is tender. Serve hot.   Serves 4.

BEANS

These recipes came from one of my best friends:
Kay Shope/Wolf Clan
CHEROKEE BEANS & *POTATOES

VENISON, CUT IN CHUNKS, (OR HAM, *optional)
WATER, OR BROTH   2-3 *POTATOES, CUBED
1 1/2 t. SALT   1 LARGE ONION, CHOPPED
1 CLOVE GARLIC, MINCED 2 YELLOW SQUASH, SLICED
1 t. PEPPER, *optional
1 1/2 C. EACH, COOKED, GREEN BEANS, KIDNEY BEANS, CRANBERRY BEANS, (*optional: BLACK-EYED PEAS, LIMA BEANS, WAX BEANS)
2 T. FRESH PARSLEY, MINCED, *optional

In large kettle, combine venison or *ham, water or broth, salt, garlic, and *pepper. Cook over medium-high heat until meat is tender. Add *potatoes, onion, squash, and beans. Simmer until potatoes and squash are tender. Stir in *parsley.   Serves 4-6.

(The best thing about this recipe is that you can keep adding things if you are feeding more people. For a real time-saver, use 15 oz. cans of beans and potatoes.)

CHEROKEE SUCCOTASH

FRESH PUMPKIN, CUT INTO SMALL PIECES
1/4 t. WILD GINGER   2 C. FRESH CORN
1/4 t. ALLSPICE   2 C. KIDNEY BEANS,
BROTH OR WATER   COOKED

In large pot, combine pumpkin, spices and broth. Boil until pumpkin is tender. Add corn and beans. Cook until completely heated.   Serves 4.

SQUASH

BAKED OR ROASTED SQUASH

This was one of the easiest ways that squash or pumpkin was prepared. Simply place it whole into the hot coals, bake until tender and skin is easily pierced. Summer squash can be eaten whole; winter squash can be cut open and the pulp eaten. Serve with maple sugar.
The squash or pumpkin was also cut in half, or in slices, and set before the fire to roast until tender.

BOILED SQUASH

Wash, peel and slice squash or pumpkin. Place into kettle, add water to cover. Add small amount of salt or 1 teaspoon maple sugar. Boil until tender. You can also add a few pieces of jerk for flavor, if desired.

BOILED SQUASH IN LEAVES

Cut squash into slices. Wrap in basswood leaves. Place in kettle with a little water and boil until tender. Remove leaves. Serve hot.

FRIED SQUASH

2-3 YELLOW OR GREEN ZUCCHINI SQUASH, SLICED
SALT
CORNMEAL
OIL OR LARD

Cut squash into thin slices. Lightly salt and coat in cornmeal. Fry in hot oil or grease until golden brown on both sides.

PUMPKIN

PUMPKIN & ONION SOUP

PUMPKIN, PEELED & DICED
ONION, SLICED
WATER

SALT
OIL OR LARD
MAPLE SUGAR

In a large pot, combine all ingredients. Boil until pumpkin is tender. Serve hot.

PUMPKIN & CORN

2 C. PUMPKIN, PEELED & DICED
3/4 C. BROTH OR WATER
1 1/2 T. OIL, OR
optional: BUTTER

1 LARGE ONION, DICED
2 C. CORN, FRESH
SALT, (PEPPER, *optional*)

In a large pot, combine pumpkin, broth or water, oil or *butter, and onion. Cover and simmer 15-20 minutes, or until pumpkin is tender. Add corn and continue simmering a few minutes longer until corn is tender. Season with salt and *pepper.   Serves 4.

PUMPKIN & PARCHED CORN STEW

PUMPKIN, PEELED & DICED
WATER
PARCHED CORN

MAPLE SUGAR
OIL OR LARD

In large kettle, combine pumpkin and water. Boil until pumpkin becomes a thin mush. Pound parched corn into a fine meal. Stir meal into pumpkin until it thickens. Add maple sugar and a small amount of lard or oil. Serve hot.

WILD RICE

1 cup of uncooked wild rice = 3-4 cups cooked wild rice.

BOILED WILD RICE

1 C. WILD RICE, RINSED & DRAINED   1 t. SALT
3-4 C. WATER, OR BROTH

In large pot, combine wild rice, water, and salt. Bring to a boil, cover, reduce heat and simmer for 40-50 minutes, or until rice is tender. Carefully drain any excess liquid, return to heat and stir until rice is dry. May be served plain or seasoned with maple sugar.   Serves 4.

WILD RICE & JERK

1 C. WILD RICE, RINSED & DRAINED   1/2 C. CHESTNUTS,
4 C. WATER   OR HAZELNUTS
1/2 C. GREEN ONIONS, SLICED   *optional:*
JERK, BROKEN IN PIECES   1 T. FRESH PARSLEY

In large pot, combine wild rice, water, onions, and jerk. Bring to a boil. Reduce heat, cover and simmer for 35 minutes. Add chopped nuts. Simmer for 15 minutes, or until rice is tender and all of the water is absorbed. Stir in *parsley.   Serves 4.

Almost anything can be cooked with wild rice:
Add fresh meat, cut in pieces, to the water and rice at the beginning. Many different vegetables, such as corn, squash, or cooked beans can also be added.

WILD RICE

PARCHED WILD RICE

1 C. WILD RICE, RINSED & DRAINED   MAPLE SUGAR
1 T. OIL OR LARD

Heat oil or lard in a heavy skillet over medium heat. Add wild rice and cook carefully, stirring constantly, until lightly browned and rice "pops" open. Remove from heat. Sprinkle maple sugar over warm rice, stir. Let cool. Eat as a snack, trail food, or breakfast cereal.

WILD RICE, NUTS & BERRIES

1 C. WILD RICE, RINSED & DRAINED   1/2 C. NUT PIECES
2 1/2 to 3 C. WATER   1/2 C. BLUEBERRIES,
1 C. GREEN ONIONS, SLICED   OR BLACKBERRIES

In large pot, combine wild rice, water and onion. Bring to a boil. Reduce heat, cover and simmer 35 minutes. Add nuts and berries. Cover and cook an additional 20 minutes, until rice is tender and all of the water is absorbed. Serve hot.   Serves 6.

(Any type of nuts can be used in this recipe. You can also use fresh or dried berries.)

ROOTS

ROASTED ONIONS

Take whole onions and place them in the hot coals of a fire. Outer skins will char, as the inside steams. Roast until tender. Remove skins, and serve.
To bake in an oven: Place large onions in an ungreased baking dish. Pour water into dish to 1/4 inch depth. Cover, cook in 350°F(180°C) oven until tender, 40-50 minutes.

ROASTED JERUSALEM ARTICHOKES

1 LB. JERUSALEM ARTICHOKES　　　　　　*OIL OR LARD*

Scrub artichokes clean. Rub lightly with oil or lard. Place into hot coals and roast for 15-20 minutes, turning occasionally. Remove from fire. Serve hot. Season with butter (**optional*).　　Serves 3-4.

CHOKES ROASTED IN LEAVES

Scrub artichokes clean. Wrap whole in green corn leaves. Use strips of husk to tie closed. Soak in water for 15 minutes. Place into hot coals and roast for 1 hour, turning occasionally, until tender. Remove leaves and serve with salt or maple sugar.

BOILED JERUSALEM ARTICHOKES

In a large kettle, place 1 pound of cleaned whole Jerusalem artichokes in enough water to cover. Boil for 10-20 minutes, or until tender. Drain and serve.　　　　　　　　　　Serves 3-4.

ROOTS

BOILED CHOKES & SQUASH

4 JERUSALEM ARTICHOKES, SLICED
3 YELLOW SQUASH, SLICED
1 MEDIUM ONION, SLICED
WATER

In medium sized kettle, combine vegetables with enough water to cover. Simmer for 30 minutes, or until vegetables are tender. Season with salt and pepper (*optional*).   Serves 3-4.

BOILED CATTAILS

Look for young cattails that have not yet sprouted the flowering stem. Pull up the center stalks. Cut off the top leaves. Remove the tough outer leaves revealing the white inner core. These can be eaten raw or placed into boiling water and simmered until tender. Serve with butter (*optional*), or season with salt.

NUTS & SEEDS

NUT MILK

Shell a quantity of nuts. Place in a mortar and pound. Add a small amount of water at a time while you are pounding. Do this until you get the consistency of milk. This is very sweet. The nut milk can be used as a flavoring for other foods or it was sometimes used as a baby formula.

(You can also use a blender or food processor.)

NUT OIL

Pound whole nuts, with their shells, in a mortar. Put into a pot with water and boil. Skim off the oil that floats to the top. Save the nut oil to use as a seasoning (like gravy) for foods like bread, squash, soups or stews. Discard the shells and drain the water. Use the nut meats as an additive to breads.

(Sunflower seeds can also be used this way.)

NUT BUTTER

Shell a quantity of nuts. Pound or grind in a mortar until nuts become a paste. Use as a flavoring for other dishes or mix with corn meal for bread.

TOASTED SEEDS

Sunflower seeds and pumpkin seeds can be toasted over a fire, in a heavy skillet, until lightly browned. They can also be toasted in the oven on baking sheets at 325°F (175°C) for 15-20 minutes.

FRUITS & BERRIES

STEWED CRANBERRIES

1 LB. FRESH CRANBERRIES, WASHED   1-2 C. WATER
1 C. MAPLE SUGAR

In large pot, combine all ingredients and simmer until cranberries pop open and are tender.   Makes about 3 cups.

(Wild cherries, as well as any other berries, can be cooked this way. Adjust sugar to taste.)

BOILED CRANBERRIES

2 C. WATER   4 C. FRESH CRANBERRIES, WASHED
2 C. MAPLE SUGAR   1/4 t. EACH GINGER, WILD ALLSPICE

In large kettle, combine water and maple sugar. Heat to boiling. Add cranberries and boil until berries pop open. Stir in ginger and allspice. Remove from heat. Serve hot or cold.

(1/2 to 1 cup of chopped nuts may also be added to either of these recipes. For a thicker sauce, stir in a small amount of cornmeal.)

STEWED PLUMS

1 C. WATER   DASH OF WILD ALLSPICE
1/2 C. MAPLE SUGAR   1 LB. PLUMS, WASHED
1/4 t. SALT

In large kettle, bring water, sugar and spices to a boil. Add plums. Cook uncovered over medium heat for 15 minutes, or until plums are tender. Remove from heat. Serve hot or cold.

FRUITS & BERRIES

DRYING FRUITS & BERRIES

To dry fruit: First cut it into thin slices, then place on a flat surface, such as a piece of cloth, flat basket, or large leaves like basswood. Place the fruit in the sun or on boards near a fire. Turn often to ensure even drying. You can also thread on strings or hang on drying racks. The drying time will vary depending upon the weather, the fire, and the type and amount of fruit you are drying.
To dry berries: Whole berries can be dried in the sun or near a fire the same as above. They will dry faster and more evenly if they are quickly blanched in boiling water first. This removes the natural wax coating on some and lightly cracks the skin on others. This allows the inside of the berry to dry.
Both fruit and berries can be dried in a dehydrator also.
Sometimes berries were first mashed into cakes and then dried. To use, these cakes can be boiled or mixed in with corn bread.

ROASTED *APPLES

Wild Crabapples were roasted whole in the hot coals of a fire until tender. Other varieties of *apples can also be cooked this way. Sometimes the simplest things can taste the best.

SPICES & SEASONINGS

MAPLE SUGAR

The sap of several varieties of maple and birch trees was used to make sugar, although the Sugar-Maple was preferred. To gather the sap, a cut was made into the bark of the tree. A wooden "spout" was driven into the cut. As the sap runs out it was gathered in birchbark or wood containers. This sap was then boiled in large kettles for hours or perhaps days, until through evaporation, it became thicker. The thickened syrup was then poured into birchbark cones or molds, and left to harden.

BEAR OIL

One of the most widely used food seasonings was Bear oil. Used much the same way as we use butter, gravy, olive oil, ketchup, syrup, etc. Basically to enhance, or add to, the flavor of almost anything. Making it was quite simple. Take the fat from a freshly butchered bear and cut it into chunks. Put it into a large kettle and simmer it until it becomes a liquid. Skim off any pieces of meat or hard "cracklings" that float to the top. Watch carefully so that it does not burn. Use caution pouring HOT oil into gourd or skin bladder container. (Optional: strain the oil through a cloth into a heat proof container.) This will keep for quite a while. Refrigerated, almost indefinitely. *Note*: Do not cook this indoors, unless you live alone (or want to). The smell of hot grease will permeate everything in your house. On the other hand, cooking it outside will bring every dog within a five mile radius. Ah well, what length won't reenactors go to?

DRIED CORNSILK

Used as a seasoning, as well as a thickening agent, cornsilk was pulled from the fresh ears of corn and placed near the fire to dry. The dried silk was then crushed into a powder. Pumpkin blossoms were also dried and used this way.

BEVERAGES

TEAS

A number of teas were made by boiling different roots, twigs or berries in water and sweetening with maple sugar. Sassafras roots, sweet birch twigs, white pine needles, red sumac berries, and rose hips were a few of the most common teas.

To make tea; bring some water to a boil. Add the roots, twigs, or berries. Return to a boil. Reduce heat and simmer for 10-15 minutes. Strain if necessary. Add maple sugar to taste, if desired.

SASSAFRAS TEA

1 T. SASSAFRAS, ROOT OR BARK   2 C. WATER

In small pot, bring water to a boil. Add sassafras and simmer for 15-20 minutes. Sweeten to taste with maple sugar, or (honey, *optional*).   Makes 2 cups.

ROSE HIP TEA

Gather a quantity of bright red rose hips (usually after the first frost). Wash and remove stems and brush ends. Place into a pot and cover with water. Simmer until hips mash easily. Add maple sugar to taste. Strain and serve.

If cooked with a smaller amount of water, you will get a concentrate. Simply add a few spoonfuls to a cup of hot or cold water, and serve.

BEVERAGES

BERRY DRINKS

Fresh berries were mashed and boiled in water, then sweetened with maple sugar if needed. This can be served hot or cold. Almost any berry could be made into a drink this way.

CRANBERRY DRINK

4 C. CRANBERRIES   6 C. WATER
2 C. MAPLE SUGAR

In medium sized pot, combine cranberries, sugar, and 1 cup of the water. Simmer until berries pop open. Mash berries and add the rest of the water. Remove from heat. Let stand for a few hours. Strain. Serve.

SUMAC-ADE

1 C. <u>RED</u> SUMAC BERRIES   1 QT. BOILING WATER

Crush sumac berries. Place in medium sized pot with boiling water. Allow to cool. Strain and serve. Sweeten with maple sugar, if desired. The taste is reminiscent of lemonade.
You can also soak a stalk of berries overnight in a pitcher of cold water. Strain and serve.

MAPLE DRINK

Stir maple sugar into cold water until completely dissolved. Keep adding sugar until you reach the desired sweetness. Serve cold.

BOTANICAL NAMES

> SOME PLANTS ARE TOXIC AT CERTAIN TIMES OF THE YEAR. **PLEASE**, MAKE SURE YOU CORRECTLY IDENTIFY EACH BEFORE COOKING OR EATING.

Acorn (*Quercus*)
Wild Allspice (*Lindera Benzoin*)
Apple (*Pyrus Malus*)
Arrowhead (*Sagittaria Latifolia*)
Bean (*Phaseolus Vulgaris*)
Beechnut (*Fagus*)
Blackberry (*Rubus Canadensis*)
Blueberry (*Vaccinium*)
Cabbage (*Brassica Oleracea*)
Carrot (*Daucus*)
Cattail (*Typha Latifolia*)
Cayenne (*Capsicum*)
Wild Cherry (*Prunus Serotina*)
Chestnut (*Castanea Sativa*)
Corn (*Zea Mays L.*)
Wild Crabapple (*Malus Coronaria*)
Cranberry (*Vaccinium Macrocarpon*)
Cucumber (*Cucumis Sativus L.*)
Dill (*Anethum Graveolens*)
Wild Garlic (*Allium Tricoccum*)
Wild Ginger (*Asarum Canadense*)
Gooseberry (*Ribes*)
Wild Grape (*Vitis Riparia*)
Groundnut (*Apios Tuberosa*)
Black Haw (*Viburnum Prunifolium*)
Red Haw (*Crataegus*)
Hazelnut (*Corylus Americana*)
Hickory nut (*Carya*)
Jerusalem Artichoke (*Helianthus Tuberosus*)
Juniper (*Juniperis Communis*)
Wild Leek (*Allium Tricoccum*)
Wild Marjoram (*Origanum Vulgare*)
Melon (*Cucumis Melo L.*)
Mint (*Mentha Arvensis*)
Mulberry (*Morus Rubra*)
Wild Onion (*Allium Textile*)
Papaw (*Asimina Triloba*)
Parsley (*Petroselinum Crispum*)
Peach (*Prunus Persica*)
Pea (*Pisum Sativum*)
Red Pepper (*Capsicum*)
Wild Plum (*Prunus Americana*)
Potato (*Solanum Tuberosum L.*)
Sweet Potato (*Ipomoea Batatas*)
Pumpkin (*Cucurbita Pepo L.*)
Black Raspberry (*Rubus*)
Red Raspberry (*Rubus Idaeus*)
Wild Rice (*Zizania Aquatica*)
Rose Hips (*Rosa*)
Sassafras (*Sassafras Albidum*)
Spicebush (*Lindera Benzoin*)
Squash (*Cucurbita Pepo*)
Strawberry (*Fragaria*)
Sugar Maple (*Acer Saccharum*)
Smooth Sumac (*Rhus Glabra*)
Staghorn Sumac (*Rhus Typhina*)
Sunflower (*Helianthus Annuus*)
Turnip (*Brassica Rapa*)
Walnut (*Juglans Nigra*)
Wheat (*Triticum Aestivum*)

BIBLIOGRAPHY

Adair, James---*Extracts from The History of the American Indians*, in *Loudon's Indian Narratives of 1808*, Reprint Ayer Publishers, N.H., 1995.
Archer, Capt. Gabriel---*Travels and works of Capt. John Smith, President of Virginia and Admiral of New England, 1580-1631*, Edward Arber, ed., Edinburgh, 1910.
Avery, George---*Journal of the Royalton Raid*, in *North Country Captives*, Colin G. Calloway, Press of New England, N.H., 1992
Bartram, John---*Observations made by...in his journey from Pennsylvania to Onondago, Oswego and the Lake Ontario in Canada*, London, 1751.
Beverly, Robert---*The History and present State of Virginia*, London, 1705.
Brown, I.W.---*Salt and the Eastern North American Indian*, Harvard University, 1980.
Brown, Thomas---*Death in the Snow, A plain narrative of the Uncommon Sufferings and Remarkable deliverance of...*, in *Captured by the Indians*, F. Drimmer, Dover Publications, N.Y., 1985.
Calloway, Colin G.---*North Country Captives, Selected Narratives of Indian Captivity from Vermont and New Hampshire*, University Press of New England, N.H., 1992
Carr, Lucien---*The food of certain American Indians and their methods of preparing it*, American Antiquarian Society proceedings, 1895.
Carver, Jonathan---*Travels through the interior parts of North America*, London, 1778.
Cox, Beverly & Jacobs, Martin---*Spirit of the Harvest, North American Indian Cooking*, Stewart, Tabori & Chang, N.Y., 1991.
Darnell, Elias---*Remember the River Raisin!*, in *Captured by the Indians*, F. Drimmer, Dover publications, 1985.
DeLong, Deanna---*How to Dry Foods*, H P Books, CA., 1992.
Densmore, Frances---*How Indians use Wild Plants for Food, Medicine and Crafts*, Dover Publications, N.Y., 1974.
Doddridge, Joseph---*Notes on the Settlement and Indian Wars...from 1763-1783*, Ritenour & Lindsey, PA., 1912.

Drake, Samuel G.---*Indian Captivities, or Life in the Wigwam*, Derby & Miller, N.Y., 1851.

Drimmer, Frederick---*Captured by the Indians, 15 Firsthand Accounts, 1750-1870*, Dover Publications, N.Y., 1985.

Eastburn, Robert---*A faithful narrative of the many dangers and sufferings, as well as wonderful and surprising deliverances of...*, in *Indian Captivities*, Samuel G. Drake, Derby & Miller, N.Y., 1851.

Fenton, William N., ed.---*Parker on the Iroquois*, Syracuse University Press, N.Y., 1968.

Ford, R.I., ed.---*An Ethnobiology Source Book, The Uses of Plants and Animals by American Indians*, Garland Publishing, 1986.

Fowler, Mary---*Captivity of...of Hopkinton in 1746*, in *North Country Captives*, C.G. Calloway, Press of New England, N.H., 1992.

Fry, Alan---*Survival in the Wilderness*, Macmillan of Canada, 1981.

Gibson, Hugh---*An account of the Captivity of...in 1756*, in *Loudon's Indian Narratives of 1808*, Reprint Ayer Publishers, N.H., 1995.

Gilbert, Benjamin---*A narrative of the Captivity and Sufferings of...in 1780*, in *Loudon's Indian Narratives of 1808*, Reprint Ayer Publishers, N.H., 1995.

Gyles, John---*The Ordeal of...Being an account of his Odd Adventures, Strange Deliverances, etc. as a Slave of the Maliseets*, Stuart Trueman, McClelland & Stewart Ltd. publishers, Canada, 1966.

Hanson, Elizabeth---*An account of the Captivity of...in 1724*, in *Indian Captivities*, Samuel G. Drake, Derby & Miller, N.Y., 1851.

Hariot, Thomas---*A Briefe and true report of the new found land of Virginia, 1585-86*, London, 1900.

Havard, Valery---*Drink Plants of the North American Indians*, Torrey Botanical Club, Bulletin 23, 1896.

Heckewelder, J.---*History, Manners, and Customs of the Indian Nations who once inhabited Pennsylvania and the neighboring states*, Historical society of Pennsylvania, 1876.

Heiser, Charles B., Jr.---*The Sunflower among the North American Indians*, American Philosophical Society, Proceedings 95, 1951.

Hennepin, Louis---*A new discovery of a vast country in America*, ed. by R.G. Thwaites, Chicago, 1903.

Henry, Alexander---*Massacre at Michilimackinac, Travels and Adventures in Canada and the Indian Territories...*, in *Captured by the Indians*, F. Drimmer, Dover Publications, N.Y., 1985.

Henry, Peter---*Accounts of his Captivity and Other Events*, in *Further Materials on Lewis Wetzel*, Heritage Books, MD., 1994.
Herbeson, Massy---*An account of the sufferings of...*, in *Indian Captivities*, Samuel G. Drake, Derby & Miller, N.Y., 1851.
How, Nehemiah---*A narrative of the captivity of...in 1745*, in *North Country Captives*, Colin G. Calloway, Press of New England, N.H., 1992.
Howe, Jemima---*The Captivity and sufferings of...*, in *North Country Captives*, Colin G. Calloway, Press of New England, N.H., 1992.
Hutchens, Alma R.---*Indian Herbalogy of North America*, Shambhala Publications, MA., 1973.
Jefferson, Thomas---*Jefferson's notes on Virginia 1781*, in *Loudon's Indian Narratives of 1808*, Reprint Ayer Publishers, N.H., 1995.
Jemison, Mary---*A narrative of the life of...*, James E. Seaver, printed for R. Parkin, London, 1826.
Johnson, Susanna---*A Narrative of the Captivity of...in 1754-57*, in *North Country Captives*, Colin G. Calloway, Press of New England, N.H., 1992.
Johnston, Charles---*Three came back*, in *Captured by the Indians*, F. Drimmer, Dover Publications, N.Y., 1985.
Johonnet, Jackson---*The Remarkable Adventure of...*, in *Loudon's Indian Narratives of 1808*, Reprint Ayer Publishers, N.H., 1995.
Josselyn, Jno.---*An account of two voyages to New England made During the years 1638-1663*, Boston, 1865.
Kalm, Peter---*Travels in North America, the English Version of 1770*, Dover Publications reprint, N.Y., 1987.
Kavasch, Barrie---*Native Harvests*, Vintage Books, 1979.
------------------------*Guide to Northeastern Wild Edibles*, Hancock House Publishers, WA., 1981.
Kindscher, K.---*Edible Wild Plants of the Prairie*, University Press of Kansas, 1987.
Knight, Dr.---*The Narrative of...*, in *Loudon's Indian Narratives of 1808*, Reprint Ayer Publishers, N.H., 1995.
Kuhnlein, H.V.---*Traditional Plant Foods of Canadian Indigenous Peoples*, Gordon & Breach Science Publishers, 1991.
Lafitau, Jos. Francois---*Moeurs des Sauvages Ameriquains*, Paris, 1724.
Lobdell, Jared C., ed.---*Further Materials on Lewis Wetzel and the Upper Ohio Frontier*, Heritage Books, MD., 1994.

Loskiel, G.H.---*History of the mission of the United Brethren among the Indians in North America,* London, 1794.

Loudon, Archibald---*Loudon's Indian Narratives of 1808,* Reprint Ayer Publishers, N.H., 1995.

Lund, Duane R.---*Early Native American Recipes and Remedies,* Adventure Publications, MN., 1989.

Lyle, Katie L.---*The Wild Berry Book, Romance, Recipes and Remedies,* North Word Press, Inc., WI., 1994.

Mahr, August C.---*Historical Reasons for the founding of Schoenbrunn,* unpublished manuscript, Ohio Historical Society, MSS #215, 1949.

McCoy, Isabella---*The Captivity of...of Epsom, N.H. in 1747,* in *North Country Captives,* Colin G. Calloway, Press of New England, N.H., 1992.

M'Cullough, John, esq.---*A Narrative of the captivity of...,* in *Loudon's Indian Narratives of 1808,* Reprint Ayer Publishers, N.H., 1995.

Morgan, Lewis H.---*League of the Iroquois,* N.Y., 1904.

Munson, Patrick J.---*Experiments and Observations on Aboriginal Wild Plant Food Utilization in Eastern North America,* Indiana Historical Society, 1984.

Noble, Frances---*Narrative of the captivity of...,* in *Indian Captivities,* Samuel G. Drake, Derby & Miller, N.Y., 1851.

Olsen, Larry D.---*Outdoor Survival Skills,* Brigham Young University Press, UT., 1973.

Palmer, Edward---*Food Products of the North American Indians,* U.S. Dept. of Agriculture, Report 15, 1870.

Parker, Arthur C.---*Iroquois uses of maize and other food plants,* New York State Educational Dept. Bulletin 482 (Museum Bulletin 144).

Percy, George---*Travels and Works of Capt. John Smith, President of Virginia and Admiral of New England, 1580-1631,* Edward Arber, ed., Edinburgh, 1910.

Peterson, Lee---*A Field Guide to the Edible Wild Plants of Eastern U.S.,* Houghton Mifflin Co., Boston, 1968.

Porcher, F.P.---*Resources of the Southern Fields and Forests, Medical, Economical, and Agricultural,* 1863.

Pouchot, Pierre---*Memoirs on the Late War in North America between France and England,* translated by Michael Cardy, Brian L. Dunnigan, ed., Old Fort Niagara Association, N.Y., 1994.

Putnam, General---*The Story of...*, in *Loudon's Indian Narratives of 1808*, Reprint Ayer Publishers, N.H., 1995.
Records, Capt. Spencer---*The Narrative of...*, in *Further Materials on Lewis Wetzel*, Heritage Books, MD., 1994.
Robison, Robert---*A narrative of...in 1757*, in *Loudon's Indian Narratives of 1808*, Reprint Ayer Publishers, N.H., 1995.
Rowlandson, Mary---*The Narrative of the Captivity and Restoration of...*, in *Indian Captivities*, Samuel G. Drake, Derby & Miller, N.Y., 1851.
Russell, Howard S.---*Indian New England Before the Mayflower*, University Press of New England, N.H., 1980.
Schuler, Stanley, ed.---*Simon & Schuster's Guide to Herbs and Spices*, Fireside, N.Y., 1990.
Scott, Francis---*A true and wonderful narrative of the surprising captivity and remarkable deliverance of...*, in *Indian Captivities*, Samuel G. Drake, Derby & Miller, N.Y., 1851.
Seaver, James E.---*A narrative of the life of Mrs. Mary Jemison*, printed for R. Parkin, London, 1826.
Sharpe, J.E. & Underwood, T.B.---*American Indian Cooking & Herb Lore*, Cherokee Publications, N.C., 1973.
Shelton, Ferne---*Pioneer Cookbook, Campfire and Kitchen Recipes from Early America*, 1973.
Slover, John---*To eat fire tomorrow*, in *Captured by the Indians*, F. Drimmer, Dover Publications, N.Y., 1985.
Smith, Col. James---*An account of the remarkable occurrences in the Life and Travels of...during his captivity with the Indians, in the years 1755-59*, in *Indian Captivities*, Samuel G. Drake, Derby & Miller, N.Y., 1851.
Spencer, O.M.---*Indian Captivity: A True Narrative of the Capture of...*, Waugh & Mason, N.Y., 1835.
Steele, Zadock---*Captivity of...*, in *North Country Captives*, Colin G. Calloway, Press of New England, N.H., 1992.
Stevens, Capt. Phineas---*Journal of...to and from Canada, 1749-1752*, in *North Country Captives*, Colin G. Calloway, Press of New England, N.H., 1992.
Stockwell, Quintin---*Narrative of the Captivity of...*, in *Indian Captivities*, Samuel G. Drake, Derby & Miller, N.Y., 1851.

Tanner, John---*The Falcon, A narrative of the Captivity & Adventures of...during Thirty Years Residence Among the Indians in the Interior of North America,* Reprint Penguin Books, N.Y., 1994.

Tantaquidgeon, Gladys---*Folk Medicine of the Delaware and related Algonkian Indians,* The Pennsylvania Historical and Museum Commission, 1972.

Trigger, Bruce G., ed.---*Handbook of North American Indians: Vol. 15, Northeast,* Smithsonian Institution, Washington D.C., 1978.

Trueman, Stuart---*The Ordeal of John Gyles,* McClelland & Stewart Ltd. Publishers, Toronto, 1966.

Van Campen, Maj. Moses---*An Inch of Ground to Fight on,* in *Captured by the Indians,* F. Drimmer, Dover Publications, N.Y., 1985.

Van den Bogaert, H.M.---*A Journey into Mohawk and Oneida Country 1634-1635,* translated & edited by C.T. Gehring & W.A. Starna, Syracuse University Press, 1988.

Vennum, Thomas---*Wild Rice and the Ojibway People,* Minnesota Historical Society Press, 1988.

Waugh, F.W.---*Iroquois foods and food preparation,* National Museums of Canada, Reprint, 1973.

Weatherford, Jack---*Indian Givers, How the Indians of the Americas transformed the World,* Crown Publishers, N.Y., 1988.

Weatherwax, Paul---*The Story of the Maize Plant,* University of Chicago, 1923.

---------------------------*Indian Corn in Old America,* Macmillan Co., N.Y., 1954.

Whisler, Frances---*Indian Cookin',* Norwega Press, 1973.

Wilber, C. Keith---*The New England Indians,* Globe Pequot Press, CT., 1978.

-------------------------*Indian Handcrafts,* Globe Pequot Press, CT., 1990.

Williamson, Peter---*A Faithful Narrative of the sufferings of...,* in *Indian Captivities,* Samuel G. Drake, Derby & Miller, N.Y., 1851.

Yanovsky, Elias---*Food plants of the North American Indians,* U.S. Dept. of Agriculture, misc. publication No.237, Wash., D.C., 1936.

NARRATIVE INDEX

A

Acorn, *see* Nuts
Adair, James *intro.*, 2, 8, 13, 22-24
Allspice, *see* Spices
Apples, *see* Fruit
Archer, Capt. Gabriel 16
Arrowhead, *see* Roots
Artichokes, *see* Roots
Ash Cakes, *see* Bread

B

Bark(s), *see* Beverages
Bay Leaf, *see* Spices
Bean(s) *intro.*, 2, 4, 7-8, 11, 13, 15-17, 19, 22, 24, 28, 35
    Cranberry 15
    Dried 15
    Green 15, 17
    Haricot 15
    Kidney *intro.*, 15, 17
    Lima 33
    Marrow 15
    Navy 15
    Parched 16
Bear, *see* Meat
Beaver, *see* Meat
Beef, *see* Meat
Berries *intro.*, 2, 13, 19, 22, 25-26, 31
    Blueberry 13, 19, 22-23, 25-26, 31
    Blackberry 25
    Cranberry 25-26, 28
    Dried 25-26
    Gooseberry 25
    Haws (Hawthorn) (Black & Red) 25-26
    Mulberry (Red) 16, 25-26
    Strawberry 25-26
    Raspberry (Black & Red) 25-26
Beechnut, *see* Nuts
Beverages
    Bark(s) *intro.*, 31
    Broth 31
    Canestalk 32
    Cornstalk 31-32
    Sumac (Red) 31
    Tea 31
    Water 8-9, 31-32
Bread 2-4, 8, 11-13, 16, 22-26, 29, 33-35
    Ash Cakes 8-9, 11-13, 15, 22, 35
    Dumplings 11-12, 15, 35
    Leaf 11, 13
    Pancake 12, 34
    Stick 34
Brown, Thomas 4
Buffalo, *see* Meat
Butter 33-34

C

Cabbage 33
Carrot(s) 33
Cattail(s), *see* Roots
Cayenne, *see* Spices
Cherry (Wild), *see* Fruit
Chestnut(s), *see* Nuts
Chicken, *see* Fowl
Chinquapin 25
Chocolate 33, 35
    Boiled 35
Clam(s) 1
Corn *intro.*, 2, 4, 6-13, 15, 17, 19, 21-24, 26-28, 31-32, 35
    Boiled 2, 4, 6, 8-10, 12-13, 15-16
    Dried 7, 11, 15-16
    Green 2, 7-8, 13, 15-16
    Hominy 4, 7-12, 15, 27, 29
    Meal 8-9, 11-13, 15, 24, 32
    Parched 7-9, 34
    Popcorn 7
    Roasted 7-8
    Silk 27
Crabapples, *see* Fruit
Crane(s), *see* Fowl
Crawfish 1, 4

81

Cucumber *intro.*, 25, 33

D
Deer, *see* Meat
Dill, *see* Spices
Duck, *see* Fowl
Eastburn, Robert 6, 15, 35
Egg(s) 1, 5
    Boiled 5
    Gull(s) 4
    Turkey 5
Elk, *see* Meat
Fish *intro.*, 1-4, 7, 16
    Boiled 2-3

    Dried 4
    Rock 4
    Shad 3
    Salmon 4
    Soup 3
    Sturgeon 4
    Trout 4
    Whitefish 4
Fowl *intro.*, 1, 4, 11, 19
    Boiled 2-3
    Duck 1, 4
    Chicken 33
    Crane(s) 4
    Goose 1, 4
    Pheasant 1
    Pigeon 1, 4-5
        Dried 4-5

    Roast 4
    Swan 4
    Turkey 1, 4-5
        Eggs 5
Frog(s) *intro.*, 5
    Dried 5
Fruit intro., 25, 33 *see also* Berries
    Apple 33-34
    Cherry (Wild) 25-26
    Crabapple 25-26
    Grape (Wild) 25
    Papaw 25

Plum (Wild) 25-26

G
Garlic, *see* Spices
Gibson, Hugh 5
Gilbert, Benjamin 2-3, 5, 7, 9,
    12, 17, 21-24, 26-27, 34
Ginger (Wild), *see* Spices
Goose, *see* Fowl
Ground Beans, *see* Roots
Ground Hog, *see* Meat
Ground Nuts, *see* Roots
Gyles, John 4

H
Hanson, Elizabeth 2, 4, 32
Hariot, Thomas 7, 24
Hawk 5-6
Heckewelder, J. *intro.*, 2, 8-9, 13,
    17, 24, 26, 28, 31
Hennepin, Louis 19
Henry, Alexander 1, 3, 8, 28
Henry, Peter 3, 12
Herb(s) 22, 24
Hickory Nut, *see* Nuts
Hominy, *see* Corn
Honey, *see* Spices
Horse, *see* Meat
How, Nehemiah 31, 35
Howe, Jemima 28

J
Jefferson, Thomas 22
Jemison, Mary 8, 15, 33, 35
Jerk, *see* Meat
    see also Venison, dried
Jerusalem Artichoke, *see* Roots
Johnson, Susanna 6, 12, 22, 29,
    34
Johnston, Charles 5, 35
Johonnet, Jackson 22
Josselyn, Jno. 15
Juniper, *see* Spices

K

Kalm, Peter *intro.*, 12, 17-19, 22-25, 29, 34
Knight, Dr. 2, 25, 29

L

Lafitau, Father 15, 32, 35
Leek (Wild), *see* Roots
Lily Root, *see* Roots
Loskiel, G.H. 31

M

Maple Sugar, *see* Spices
Marjoram (Wild), *see* Spices

Marten 1
McCoy, Mrs. 33
M'Cullough, John 7-8, 11-12, 17, 21, 26, 29, 33
Meat 1-4, 7-8, 15, 18-19, 22, 24, 28, 31, 33-34
    Bear *intro.*, 1, 3-5, 12, 15, 22, 28
        Boiled 5
        Dried 28
        Liver 5
        Oil 1-3, 12-13, 27-29, 34
        Roast 5
    Beaver *intro.*, 1-2, 6

        Boiled 6
    Beef 33, 35
        Roast 35
    Buffalo *intro.*, 1-3, 5, 29
        Boiled 2
        Dried 18
        Tongue 5

    Deer 1-3, 5-6, 28 *see also* Venison
        Blood 6
    Elk 1, 3
    Ground Hog 2, 27
    Horse 6, 31
        Boiled 32
        Dried 6
    Jerk 1-3, 6, 25 *see also* Venison, dried
    Moose 1-2

    Muskrat 2, 6
    Otter 2-3
    Pork 33-35
    Rabbit *intro.*, 1-3, 23

    Raccoon 1
    Squirrel *intro.*, 1-2
Milk 33
Milkweed 5
Mint, *see* Spices
Moose, *see* Meat

Muskrat, *See* Meat
Mussel(s) 1

N

Noble, Frances 28
Nut(s) *intro.*, 2, 8, 19, 21, 23-26
    Acorn 21, 23
    Beechnut 23
    Butter 23
    Chestnut 8, 13, 23, 25
    Hazelnut 23, 25
    Hickory nut 8, 23-25
    Milk 23-24, 32
    Oil 24
    Walnut (Black) 23-26, 32

O

Onion, *see* Roots
Otter, *see* Meat
Oil, Bear, *see* Meat
    Nut, *see* Nuts
Oregano, *see* Spices

P

Pancake, *see* Bread
Papaw, *see* Fruit
Paprika, *see* Spices
Parsley, *see* Spices
Pea(s) 22, 24, 33, 35
Peach, *see* Fruit
Pepper, *see* Spices
Percy, George 11

Pheasant, *see* Fowl
Pigeon, *see* Fowl
Popcorn, *see* Corn
Pork, *see* Meat
Potato *intro*.
    Swamp, *see* Arrowhead
    Sweet 33
Pumpkin, *see* Squash

R
Rabbit, *see* Meat
Raccoon, *see* Meat
Radisson, Pierre 19
Records, Capt. Spencer 3, 31, 35
Red Pepper, *see* Spices
Robison, Robert 26
Roots *intro*., 2, 21, 22, 24-26, 29, 31
    Arrowhead (Swamp Potato) 21-22, 34
    Boiled 21-22
    Cattails 21
    Dried 21
    Ground Beans 21
    Groundnut 21-22, 34-35
        Cake 22
    Jerusalem Artichoke 21
    Leek (Wild) 21
    Onion 21-22
Rowlandson, Mary *intro*., 6, 8, 16, 21-23, 32, 34-35

S
Sage, *see* Spices
Salt, *see* Spices
Sassafras, *see* Spices
Scott, Mrs. Frances 32
Seeds 23
    Pumpkin 23
    Squash 23
    Sunflower 15, 23
    Toasted 23
Slover, John 4
Smith, Col. James *intro*., 1-5, 8, 11, 15, 18-19, 21, 23, 25-29, 35

Soup 1, 3, 5, 8, 11, 22-23, 25, 29, 31-32
Spencer, O.M. 2, 5, 7, 9-10, 13, 16 26-28, 31
Spicebush, *see* Spices
Spices 17, 23, 27, 29
    Bay Leaf 33
    Dill 33
    Garlic 27
    Ginger (Wild) 27, 29

    Honey 33, 35
    Juniper 27
    Maple Sugar 1, 8-9, 13, 18, 26-29, 31, 35
    Marjoram (Wild) 27
    Oregano 27
    Parsley 33
    Red Pepper 27, 29
        Cayenne 27, 29
        Paprika 27, 29
    Salt 2-3, 13, 27, 29, 35
    Sassafras 31-32
    Spicebush (Wild Allspice) 27, 31
    Sugar 35
Squash *intro*., 2, 7, 17-19, 22-23
    Acorn 17
    Boiled 17-18
    Crookneck 17
    Dried 17-18
    Pumpkin *intro*., 2, 8, 12-13 15-18, 22-24
        Boiled 17-18
        Dried 18
        Roasted 2, 18
    Roasted 17
    Scalloped 17
    Straightneck 17
    Zucchini (Green) 17
Squirrel, *see* Meat
Steele, Zadock 16, 22, 34
Stew 1-3, 11, 25
Stockwell, Quintin 2-3
Sunflower 15, 23 *see also* Seeds

Swan(s), *see* Fowl

T
Tanner, John 2-5, 23, 27
Trout, *see* Fish
Turkey, *see* Fowl
Turnips 17, 22, 33-34
Turtle *intro.*, 1, 26

V
Van Campen, Major Moses 4
Van den Bogaert, H.M. 4, 11, 15, 17, 23, 26
Vegetables 19
Venison 2-3, 17, 21, 24, 28
    Boiled 1-2, 5
    Broiled 1-2
    Dried 1, 3, 8, 13, 28, 29
        see also Jerk
    Roasted 1-2, 8, 28
    Stewed 2

W
Walnut, *see* Nuts
Water, *see* Beverages
Watermelon 15, 33
Wild Rice *intro.*, 19
    Boiled 19
    Dried 19
    Parched 19
Williamson, Peter 7

Z
Zucchini (Green), *see* Squash

RECIPE INDEX

BEANS
Another "Brunswick" Stew 47
Beans & Squash 58
Boiled Corn Bread 53
Cherokee Beans & Potatoes 59
Cherokee Succotash 59
Corn Bread 48
Corn & Beans 48
Cranberry Beans & Corn 57
Dried Bean Soup 57
Fish & Corn Soup 46
Green Beans & Jerk 57
Hominy Soup 49
Hominy & Sunflower Soup 50
Jerk & Beans 44
Meat, Squash & Bean Soup 58
Sweet Bean Soup 58

BEVERAGES
Berry Drinks 71
Cranberry Drink 71
Maple Drink 71
Rose Hip Tea 70
Sassafras Tea 70
Sumac-ade 71
Teas 70

BREAD
Ash Cakes 53
Boiled Corn Bread 53
Corn Bread 48
Corn, Pumpkin & Berry Cakes 54
Cranberry Dumplings 54
Green Corn Bread 56
Hominy Pancakes 54
Leaf Bread 55
Leaf Bread with Meat 55
Leaf Nut Bread 55
Pumpkin Bread 56

CORN
Another "Brunswick" Stew 47
Cherokee Succotash 59
Corn & Beans 48

CORN cont.
Corn & Duck Stew 48
Cranberry Beans & Corn 57
Dried Hominy 49
Elk Stew 40
Fish Soup 46
Fish & Corn Soup 46
Hominy Soup 49
Hominy & Sunflower Soup 50
Jerk Soup 44
Making Hominy 49
Making Parched Corn 51
Nut Butter Hominy 50
Parched Corn 51
Popcorn Mush 52
Popcorn Soup 52
Pumpkin & Corn 61
Pumpkin & Parched Corn Stew 61
Turkey & Corn Stew 47
Venison & Corn Soup 39
Wild Rice (Stir in) 62
Yes, Popcorn 52

DRYING
Dehydrator 38
    Meat & Produce
Oven 38
    Meat & Produce
Sun 38
    Produce

FISH
Boiled Fish 45
Boiled Fish & Potatoes 45
Dried & Smoked Fish 46
Fish Soup 46
Fish & Corn Soup 46
Roast Fish 45
Roasted Stuffed Fish 45

FOWL
Another "Brunswick" Stew 47
Corn & Duck Stew 48
Turkey & Corn Stew 47

FRUITS & BERRIES
Boiled Corn Bread 53
Boiled Cranberries 67
Corn Bread 53
Corn, Pumpkin & Berry Cakes 54
Cranberry Dumplings 54
Drying Fruits & Berries 68
Green Corn Bread 56
Hominy Soup 49
Meat & Berry Soup 41
Pumpkin Bread 56
Roasted Apples 68
Stewed Cranberries 67
Stewed Plums 67
Wild Rice, Nuts & Berries 63

HELPFUL HINTS
Presoaking Dried Beans 38
Hominy 38
Vegetables 38

MEAT
Buffalo & Wild Rice 40
Deer Liver & Onions 41
Elk Stew 40
Jerk Soup 44
Jerk & Beans 44
Making Jerk 43
Meat & Berry Soup 41
Modern Jerk Marinade 44
Rabbit & Wild Rice 42
Roast Rabbit 42
Roasting Meat 39
Venison Roast 39
Venison & Corn Soup 39

NUTS & SEEDS
Boiled Corn Bread 53
Buffalo & Wild Rice 40
Corn Bread 53
Corn & Duck Stew 48
Green Corn Bread 56
Hominy Soup 49
Hominy & Sunflower Soup 50
Leaf Nut Bread 55
Nut Butter 66

NUTS & SEEDS *cont.*
Nut Butter Hominy 50
Nut Milk 66
Nut Oil 66
Pumpkin Bread 56
Rabbit & Wild Rice 42
Toasted Seeds 66
Wild Rice & Jerk 62
Wild Rice, Nuts & Berries 63

ROOTS
Another "Brunswick" Stew 47
Beans & Squash 58
Boiled Cattails 65
Boiled Chokes & Squash 65
Boiled Corn Bread 53
Boiled Fish & Potatoes 45
Boiled Jerusalem Artichokes 64
Buffalo & Wild Rice 40
Cherokee Beans & Potatoes 59
Chokes Roasted in Leaves 64
Corn & Duck Stew 48
Deer Liver & Onions 41
Elk Stew 40
Fish & Corn Soup 46
Hominy Soup 49
Hominy & Sunflower Soup 50
Jerk Soup 44
Jerk & Beans 44
Leaf Bread with Meat 55
Meat & Berry Soup 41
Popcorn Soup 52
Pumpkin & Corn 61
Pumpkin & Onion Soup 61
Rabbit & Wild Rice 42
Roasted Jerusalem Artichokes 64
Roasted Onions 64
Roasted Stuffed Fish 45
Turkey & Corn Stew 47
Venison Roast 39
Venison & Corn Soup 39
Wild Rice & Jerk 62
Wild Rice, Nuts & Berries 63

SPICES & SEASONINGS
Allspice 56, 59, 67
Bay Leaf 40, 45, 47
Bear Oil 48-49, 57
    Making 69
Butter 64-65
Cayenne 39, 42-44, 47, 55, 58
Dill 44
Dried Cornsilk 40
    Making 69
Garlic 44-45
Ginger 58-59, 67
Honey 49, 52, 54, 70
Liquid Smoke 43, 46
Maple Sugar 41, 48-54, 57-58, 60-64, 67, 70-71
Making 69
Marjoram (Wild) 58
Nut Butter 66
    Milk 66
    Oil 66
Oregano 47, 58
Paprika 42-44, 47
Parsley 46-47, 59, 62
Pepper 44, 46-47, 59, 61, 64
Sage 40-41
Salt 39-46, 48-62, 64-65, 67
Sugar 43

SQUASH & PUMPKINS
Baked or Roasted Squash 60
Beans & Squash 58
Boiled Chokes & Squash 65
Boiled Corn Bread 53
Boiled Squash 60
Boiled Squash in Leaves 60
Cherokee Beans & Potatoes 59
Cherokee Succotash 59
Corn Bread 53
Corn, Pumpkin & Berry Cakes 54
Elk Stew 40
Fried Squash 60
Hominy Soup 49
Jerk Soup 44
Meat, Squash & Bean Soup 58
Pumpkin Bread 56

SQUASH & PUMPKINS *cont.*
Pumpkin & Corn 61
Pumpkin & Onion Soup 61
Pumpkin & Parched Corn Stew 61
Roasted Stuffed Fish 45
Wild Rice (Stir in) 62

SUBSTITUTIONS
For:
    Bear Oil 38
    Buffalo 38
    Elk 38
    Maple Sugar 38
    Venison 38

WILD RICE
Boiled Wild Rice 62
Buffalo & Wild Rice 40
Parched Wild Rice 63
Rabbit & Wild Rice 42
Roasted Stuffed Fish 45
Wild Rice & Jerk 62
Wild Rice, Nuts & Berries 63

NOTES

About the Author:
Carolyn Raine, of Seneca heritage, is a full-time artist and historian. She has been a historical reenactor for the last 15 years. She runs a small business, "Spirit of the Forest", specializing in all aspects of 18th century Native American culture. Carolyn can often be found at historic sites, giving seminars and demonstrations on traditional 18th century lifestyles, including Native history and art, as well as, foods and food preparation.